Photograph by Rob Paris

MABEL MORSBACH grew up in Cincinnati, where she attended the public schools. She was graduated from Furman University in Greenville, South Carolina, and then returned to Ohio to do graduate work at the University of Cincinnati.

She taught language arts and social studies to fifth-grade classes in the Cincinnati Public Schools until 1959. At that time she accepted a special assignment to write a history of the city of Cincinnati for use in the fifth grade. The book that resulted, *We Live in Cincinnati,* was published in 1961 and is used as a text in the public schools of that city. She has also written a book for junior and senior high school use, *Teaching About Communism.*

In addition to writing, Miss Morsbach has done work in curriculum development. She has also been employed in educational television, serving as a teacher of a language arts-social studies telecourse for grades four through six. At the present time she is supervising teacher in the Department of Instruction of the Cincinnati Public Schools.

The Negro in American Life

Original edition published by the Cincinnati Board of Education.
This edition published under a license from The John J. Murphy Company of
Cincinnati, Ohio, by Harcourt, Brace & World.

The Negro in American Life

Mabel Morsbach

Harcourt, Brace & World, Inc.   New York

Curriculum-Related Books, selected and edited by the School Department of Harcourt, Brace & World, are titles of general interest for individual reading.

Acknowledgments

The Cincinnati Public Schools acknowledge the contributions of many individuals who helped in the preparation of the first edition of this book.

Special recognition is given to Dr. Gustav G. Carlson, Head of the Department of Sociology and Anthropology, University of Cincinnati, for his significant help in writing the introductory chapter and for his assistance in reading the entire manuscript.

For criticism and evaluation: Mrs. Vivian Beamon, Principal, Hays School and President, Urban League of Greater Cincinnati; William A. DuPree, Teacher, Ach Junior High School; Dr. Louis R. Harlan, Professor of History, University of Cincinnati; Miss Leonore Holliday, Teacher, Gamble Junior High School; Mrs. Laura Lovelace, Principal, Rockdale School; Mrs. Virginia M. Lutton, Teacher, Porter Junior High School; Dr. Harold S. Smith, Professor of History, Kentucky State College; Donald P. Sowell, Supervisor of Art Education; Roger Tilford, Teacher, Ach Junior High School; Paul A. Trinkle, Teacher, Eastern Hills Junior High School; Dr. Charles H. Wesley, Former President, Central State College.

For advice and guidance: Dr. Rufus Atwood, Chairman, Education Committee, Cincinnati Chapter, National Association for the Advancement of Colored People; The Reverend L. Venchael Booth, Pastor, Zion Baptist Church; Dr. Paul Browning, Director, Education and Youth Incentives, Urban League; Malcolm Chandler, Executive Director, National Conference of Christians and Jews; Joseph Hall, Executive Director, Urban League of Greater Cincinnati; Mrs. Joan Nicholas, Committee Chairman, Negro History Study Group, North Avondale Neighborhood Association; Mrs. Mary Schloss, President, Ohio Congress of Parents and Teachers; Ralph E. Shauck, Director of Secondary Education, Cincinnati Public Schools; Miss Jean Tilford, Supervisor of Social Studies, Cincinnati Public Schools; Miss Helen Yeager, Supervisor of Social Studies, Cincinnati Public Schools.

Appreciation is gratefully expressed to all persons who had a part in the planning and publishing of this book.

ROBERT P. CURRY
Associate Superintendent
Cincinnati Public Schools

Picture Credits

Title Page: Harbrace Photo; p. 2, Library of Congress; p. 14, The Museum of Primitive Art; p. 16, Harbrace Map; p. 18, Map Division, New York Public Library; p. 23, The Museum of Primitive Art; p. 24, The Museum of Primitive Art; p. 26, Culver Pictures, Inc.; p. 29, Harbrace Map; p. 35, The New York Historical Society; p. 38, Brown Brothers; p. 47, Chicago Historical Society; p. 51, Culver Pictures, Inc.; p. 59, Library of Congress; p. 64, Illustrated London News; p. 69, Harbrace Map; p. 71, The New York Historical Society; p. 80, Library of Congress; p. 82, Library of Congress; p. 90, Library of Congress; p. 101, Gumby Collection, Columbia University; p. 103, Library of Congress; p. 107–108, Library of Congress; p. 110, Collection, The Museum of Modern Art, New York; p. 112, Library of Congress; p. 117, Harper's Weekly; p. 128, Elliott Erwitt, Magnum; p. 130, Library of Congress; p. 135, Underwood & Underwood; p. 138, Underwood & Underwood; p. 144–45, Cincinnati Art Museum; p. 148, Gumby Collection, Columbia University; p. 152, Allen Art Museum, Oberlin, Ohio; p. 155, Brown Brothers; p. 157, Gumby Collection, Columbia University; p. 159, Brown Brothers; p. 162, Gumby Collection, Columbia University; p. 165, Underwood & Underwood; p. 167, Underwood & Underwood; p. 169, Culver Pictures, Inc.; p. 174–75, The Detroit Institute of Arts; p. 179; Hurok Attractions; p. 190, Underwood & Underwood; p. 196, UPI; p. 202, UPI; p. 204, UPI; p. 208, UPI; p. 214, UPI; p. 215, UPI; p. 221, UPI; p. 225, Underwood & Underwood; p. 227, UPI; p. 233, UPI; p. 239, UPI; p. 242, UPI.

Foreword

Our nation, made up of persons with many different racial, religious, and national origins, has developed its unique culture through the individual and group contributions of all its citizens. The variety of multiracial and multiethnic backgrounds has enriched our culture. The same variety has also made it imperative to promote positive human understandings so that citizens may live together harmoniously, with mutual respect for the achievements of all.

Recognition and appreciation of contributions of these various racial and ethnic groups should be based on accurate knowledge. In the study of American history, however, pupils often have difficulty in finding adequate information about the role of minority groups in the development of their country. Textbooks, for example, generally include an incomplete treatment of the influence of Negroes upon American life. Recognition of Negro contributions is usually limited to certain periods of American history, with little mention of this group's continuing involvement in America's growth.

The Negro in American Life was instigated and developed under the general direction of Robert P. Curry, Associate Superintendent, Cincinnati Public Schools, to supplement the inadequate information presented in most texts and to supply pupils with a broader picture of Negro participation in the progress of our nation. The book aims to set forth the historical significance and achievements of Negroes, both individually and as a group, from the age of exploration to modern times. While it highlights Negro influence throughout the sweep of American history, it does not attempt to present an exhaustive account of Negro life.

It seeks, rather, to show the interplay between important historical forces and the degree of Negro involvement in American life.

The Negro in American Life is designed for use in classes in American history. Since it is to complement material presented in adopted history textbooks, it is organized in a chronological order. The correlated study of Negro contributions within the framework of the historical development of the United States should enrich the pupils' appreciation for the role of minorities in the growth of American progress.

It is hoped that this book will be useful in promoting harmonious intergroup understanding. Young people who read about the success of individuals who overcame obstacles in the past may be inspired to meet the challenges of today's world courageously. They may realize anew that the social, economic, and political progress of the United States has evolved from the combined efforts of many citizens of diverse racial and ethnic backgrounds. They may be led to a deeper awareness that since they have inherited a free society, they, too, have a responsibility for working cooperatively with all people to strengthen the ideals of the American heritage.

WENDELL H. PIERCE

September, 1966   Superintendent of Schools
                                   Cincinnati Public Schools

Contents

The Negro in American Life

Introduction

*Here is not merely a nation, but
a teeming Nation of nations.*
　　　　　　—WALT WHITMAN

Pluralism, the mingling of many, is one of the most conspicuous features of American life. The late President John F. Kennedy called attention to it by referring to our country as a "nation of immigrants." This pluralism has enriched American life. It is reflected in a wide variety of customs, traditions, and religious doctrines.

The actuality of pluralism in our country can be seen by looking at a few figures. In 1960, among the 179,323,175 people in the United States, there were

158,832,000 Whites
> (This figure includes the Jewish population.)

18,872,000 Negroes
> (Negroes made up 92 percent of all non-Whites.)

1,620,000 Other non-Whites
> (Non-Whites include American Indians, Japanese, Chinese, Filipinos, and those born of mixed parentage.)

9,738,000 Foreign-born

5,531,000 Jews

3

Poor but free European immigrants of New York, late 1800's.

Pluralism, The Result of Immigration

Immigration has had a continuing effect on our country from its very discovery. Every American, past or present, has been either an immigrant or a descendant of immigrants. Even the "native" Indians were migrants. Anthropologists are agreed that they were the country's first settlers, coming here from Asia.

Why did America attract many thousands of newcomers? It held out the hope of a better life, a new start. Some of the earliest immigrants were seeking religious freedom. Others came hoping to find a greater share of wealth, and still others were searching for political freedom. Most newcomers came to America with visions of greater opportunity for themselves and their children. As they faced the future in a new land, they learned to get along in a new environment. They lived through unfamiliar experiences while working and living among Americans whose customs often seemed strange. The life of each immigrant was changed by the impact of his new surroundings. Each group, moreover, brought different traditions and cultures, some of which became part of American life.

There have been two main periods of immigration in our country. The early period spanned colonial times when people from several nations came to build settlements in the American wilderness. The second major period of immigration began in the early 1800's and continued through the first two decades of the 1900's.

The First Period of Immigration

The early immigrants had to overcome many hardships to establish homes in an unsettled country. Building shelters, getting food, making clothing, finding fuel—these were just a few of the problems that the first immigrants solved through their own efforts.

In the thirteen original colonies, the majority of immigrants came from Great Britain. Because they were the first arrivals, they were able to establish many of their familiar British customs in the new land. They laid the foundations for a common language, type of government, and a system of law. No other group that followed would be able to transfer so many of its national traditions.

Manpower was urgently needed to build and safeguard the colonies, and for that reason immigrants from other nations were welcomed as settlers. The Dutch built their strong, solid homes in New Amsterdam and along the Hudson Valley. Polish and Italian craftsmen lived in Jamestown. The Swedes, living mainly in Delaware, were the first to build log cabins in the New World. A small group of people from Wales settled in Pennsylvania. A sprinkling of Germans, Swiss, and French were found in several of the colonies. Adventurous folk from Scotland and Ireland pushed out to the edge of the frontier to make their homes. African captives, unwilling immigrants, to be sure, also lived and worked in the colonies. Thus, from its earliest days of settlement, America was a mixture of different groups of people with a variety of backgrounds.

The Second Period of Immigration

During the period of a little more than 100 years, from the early nineteenth century to the early twentieth century, there were great waves of immigration to the United States. One of the first groups to reach our country in large numbers was the Irish.

Repeated failures of their potato crop, a major source of food in Ireland, resulted in a period of famine during the 1840's. Faced by the frightening possibility of starving, Irish peasants by the thousands sailed to the United States. Unlike the earlier colonial immigrants, the Irish came to a land already settled. Their experience of adjusting to a new but settled country was similar to that of many groups who came later. In the eyes of the settled Americans, the Irish immigrants were poor, unskilled, and different in their speech and dress. They were outsiders. These bewildered newcomers experienced hardships caused by a discrimination that shut them off from many opportunities. For example, help-wanted ads often stated, "No Irish need apply." In spite of prejudice and discrimination, the Irish managed to surmount obstacles and to take advantage of opportunities. Through their work and determination, they were able to give their children greater advantages than they themselves had found. As the years passed, their children and grandchildren were absorbed into the American pattern of life.

After the Irish, came the Germans. More people have come to the United States from Germany than from any other country. Between 1830 and 1930, approximately six million Germans came to America to live. Large numbers of them settled in Cincinnati, Baltimore, St. Louis, Minneapolis, and Milwaukee. Skilled German workmen made fine pianos and organs and then enjoyed the German music played on them. Sauerbraten and potato pancakes are served today in the restaurants of these cities, and beer brewed by the descendants of Germans is sold across the country.

During the middle years of the 1800's, there was a large influx of immigrants from Scandinavia. The largest number came from Sweden, but a little later there were many from Norway and Denmark as well. Most of the Scandinavians settled in Minnesota and Michigan.

During the 1880's there came a large wave of Italians, five million of them. By the turn of the century, groups were arriving from other European countries. There were Russians, Poles, Jews, Hungarians, Czechs, Rumanians, Bulgarians, Austrians, and Greeks. To the already settled Americans, these newcomers presented a bewildering assortment of strange languages and customs that seemed impossible to understand. The migrations continued. From eastern Europe came other groups from Latvia, Lithuania, Turkey, and Armenia.

In the late 1800's, immigrants came also from Oriental countries and settled along the west coast. The Chinese came after the 1860's and helped build the Central Pacific Railroad. Some Japanese came toward the turn of the century. The Orientals were truly outsiders. Coming from a markedly different background, they had unhappy experiences with extreme prejudice and discrimination. In more recent times, immigrants have traveled shorter distances to reach the United States. These newcomers have arrived from Mexico, Puerto Rico, and Cuba.

Each new wave of immigrants encountered some degree of hostility from the settled Americans. As the newcomers adjusted to life in the United States, many of their former habits and customs were forgotten; but some of the ways they brought with them have become American customs.

Minorities, Prejudice, and Discrimination

A minority is a group of people who are different from the majority of the citizens in either their physical appearance or their culture. Most minority groups in America identify themselves by race, national origin, or religion. Prejudice enters the picture when individuals of a minority group face disapproval or dislike for reasons having nothing to do with their personalities or characters, but simply because of their membership in a minority group. Prejudice involves bad feeling, but not action. Discrimination, on the other hand, is action. One can think of discrimination as the acting out of prejudice. Most of the various racial or ethnic groups in America have experienced both prejudice and discrimination at one time or another. Opportunities have also been closed to many talented individuals of religious and racial minorities. Until 1960, no Catholic was ever elected President of the United States. Even during Mr. Kennedy's campaign for election, some experts felt that prejudice against his Catholic background might defeat his hopes for success.

While all minority groups have experienced some degree of prejudice, perhaps the sharpest hostility has been directed at easily identifiable racial groups. The hostility shows itself in discrimination, and the members of these racially different groups tend to remain longer outside the mainstream of society in isolated groups of their own people. And, in a circular way, they are then considered even more isolated and different by the majority—so that a Japanese or Negro who was born and has lived his entire life in this country is frequently not referred to simply as an *American*. He is called a Japanese or a Negro and is set apart from the mainstream of American life.

The experiences of different minority groups in our country have varied. To try to understand why prejudices developed, let us consider the experiences of three groups—the Indians, the later European immigrants, and the Negroes.

The Indians

When early colonists landed in the New World, they were impressed by the vast stretches of unoccupied land. The newcomers soon discovered that it was not as free as it seemed. The Indians had claims on the land. It was either their homeland or their hunting grounds, and they were prepared to fight in its defense.

Larger numbers of settlers pouring into the colonies required more and more land. They took it. To the Indians, this was a clear invasion of their territory, and they took to the warpath to protect their land. Colonists spoke grimly of the Indian problem. They realized that the Indians must be conquered before colonial settlements would be safe. In frontier skirmishes, many Indians were overthrown and pushed out of their long-established territories. Thousands were killed, too.

During this period of strife, an excuse to justify fighting the Indians was developed. The blame must be placed on the minority group, if the majority group is to feel blameless. The idea developed and became widespread that Indians were treacherous, murdering savages. All Indians were described in this manner. Because settlers accepted this description as truth, they convinced themselves that they were fighting only to protect their homes from "murderous savages." They lost sight of the fact that the Indian, too, was fighting for his homeland and that it was the settlers themselves who were the invaders.

As the frontier was pushed inland, the Indians had less and less space in which to live. The solution that was chosen was reservation living, and, as a conquered people, the Indians had to accept this way of life. Even today, the majority of Indians remain separated from other Americans.

European Immigrants

Most of the immigrants who came to the United States in the 1800's were in desperate need. Even before they landed, they had suffered through several crises and their hardships were far from over.

Mainly farmers or craftsmen, the immigrants had lived in the same small villages or towns as their fathers and grandfathers before them. Unaccustomed to change, they had farmed their small plots of land or worked at their trades in the traditional ways. When the farm or the trade no longer provided enough income, they decided to migrate to America. From that moment, old habits were broken, and changes came rapidly into their once serene lives. Their few possessions were either packed or sold. They journeyed to a seacoast town, most of them by foot. Once there, arrangements were made to get passage on a boat. The period of waiting for a boat to sail varied. Some waited only a few days, others, months.

Once on a ship, the immigrant and his family lived for about forty days in the overcrowded steerage section, below decks. Cold and dirty, the cramped quarters were home to people and rats alike. Poor water, scarce food, and disease added to the misery. Approximately one immigrant out of ten never reached his destination.

Upon arrival in the United States, most of the migrants had little money. They had to find work immediately, or go hungry. Because of this they took any jobs they could get. They accepted low pay and made no objections to poor working conditions or long hours. Because of his great need, the newcomer did the most menial jobs with the longest hours.

Adjusting to American life was not easy. The land was already settled, and customs were rather firmly set. The immigrant was the outsider, the stranger. His language was different; his clothing looked odd. His farm-centered habits were no longer helpful in the big city. Everything to which he was accustomed seemed wrong or useless in the new land. He would need to learn new skills and habits to exist in his adopted country.

There was comfort in living close to others from his own home-land. The newcomers crowded into cheap tenements where others spoke the same language and had the same memories. There some of the old traditions were kept alive at the same time as new ways of living and working were being developed.

As the immigrant family stayed in the United States, it grad-ually took on some of the customs of the country and became "Americanized." In time, the wage-earner found a better job. He moved from his first crowded apartment to a better or larger one. His children, who adjusted more easily than their parents, were quicker to understand and follow the American ways.

Each new wave of immigrants passed through the same cycle. Each new group arrived with desperate needs. For a while, they had the poorest homes, the most menial jobs, and the longest working hours. As time passed, their position improved. They or their children were fully accepted by other Americans. They lost their national identity and left behind their minority group status and the prejudice accompanying such a status and entered into the main current of American life.

The Negroes

The experience of the Negro in the United States was not like that of the other immigrants. Everything about his situation was unique. To start with, his darker color and racial features were biological, not cultural, differences and so he could not, like mem-bers of other minorities, lose his external identity. While all other immigrants chose to come to America, almost all but the first Africans were brought as captives against their wills. As slaves, they were forced to abandon the customs of their native land. They had to adjust quickly to the demands of a new pattern of living.

Unlike the European immigrants, who usually spent only a short time in the most menial jobs, the African slaves were trapped in a permanent laboring class. No matter how skillful a slave was, his chances for improving his living conditions were slight. His life in the New World was a backward step instead of the forward step that it was for the immigrants.

Hardships of Slavery. There were hardships that slaves endured other than being permanently bound to menial labor. They had no control over their home lives. Where they lived depended entirely upon who bought them. They had no part in choosing a home—they only accepted whatever shelter was provided. Whether or not families remained together depended upon their owners, who had the power to sell single members of the slave family to separate owners. Slave parents could do nothing to pro-

Negroes at a slave auction, about to be sold as property.

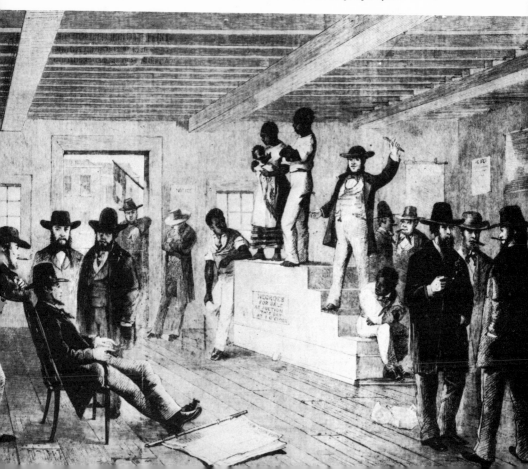

tect their children or themselves from these separations. Indeed, slave parents had little responsibility in raising their children. It was the owners who provided food, clothing, and training for future work.

Other responsibilities were withheld from the slaves. Trained to be obedient, they were discouraged from making decisions of their own or from learning to read. With any education, slaves might become discontented with their lot. The slave was treated as a backward child. Without a chance to get an education, he was called stupid. Punished if he acted on his own decisions, he was called irresponsible. Although he had no chance to use or develop his talents, he was called inferior. Owners came to believe their slaves were all the things they called them.

The slave experience had a marked influence upon the Negro's position in America. Many of the prejudices which were born in those early days remained. Custom, fear, and, in some cases, the law shut doors of opportunity. Negroes form the largest minority group in America, yet they have had the longest struggle against barriers of discrimination. In recent years, significant progress has been made in correcting some of the injustices of the past. Changing conditions in the United States and in the world have forced our country to take a new look at the role of the Negro in American life.

Negroes as a Minority. Prejudice and the discrimination that results from it have many roots. Ignorance is certainly one. Because a minority is generally considered inferior, accurate information about the group is often scarce. Few people in the United States, for example, realize the full extent of Negro contributions to American life. Negroes have made outstanding records in many areas of our national life. Books written by Negro authors have been translated into other languages and are read in other countries. The voices of some have been heard in concert halls throughout the world. Paintings of others hang in art museums in our country and abroad. Entertainers have been sent as ambassadors of good will around the world and even into the Soviet Union.

Athletes have set records in international sports events. Doctors, including one who developed a process of reducing blood to plasma, which saved hundreds of thousands of lives in World War II, save lives and improve health every day. In every profession, there have been talented Negroes whose contributions have advanced America's well-being.

Negro citizens today, taking advantage of greater opportunities, are employed in many different kinds of occupations. As a result, there has been increasing diversity in the life of the Negro community. Many Negroes live in rural areas and earn their living by farming. Many others live in large cities and work in factories, stores, offices, and restaurants. Some individuals work in the field of education as teachers, principals, or college professors. Others are lawyers, doctors, nurses, or social workers. Negro policemen protect city dwellers, and Negro soldiers and sailors strengthen the United States armed forces. Ambassadors and members of the Peace Corps serve their country by working in foreign countries. In ever-increasing numbers, young people are preparing for future careers by attending college. Thousands of Negroes in the United States live on low incomes like many other citizens. Thousands of others have comfortable standards of living and some are wealthy. Like other Americans, Negroes range from laborers to owners of factories, from minor entertainers to well-known stars, from privates in the Army to high ranking officers, and from government clerks to elected officials on local and national levels.

Negroes in America have followed a course different from that of the immigrants who sailed here to start new, happier lives. Most of them were brought against their wills, to be slaves. During the period of slavery, a number of free Negroes shared in the life of American society, but it was not until after the Civil War, during which slavery was abolished, that most Negroes began to enter into American life as full citizens.

The African Background

The history of the Negro race stretches far backward in time. For many centuries before America was discovered, the African people had been developing their own unique customs, traditions, and skills. They were the background that the Negro captive brought with him to the Americas, though he was often forced to forget these traditions.

When Africans were brought to the New World as slaves, their masters knew little about their homeland or customs. Whether or not the newly bought slave had once been the ruler of a village state was unimportant. His whole past life, in fact, was unimportant to his owner. Only his future life of labor mattered.

Studies of African history show that some complex ways of living had been developed there. While life was primitive in some areas, there were other sections with remarkably well-organized states and kingdoms. West Africa, for example, had developed magnificent, wealthy empires, and it was from West Africa that the majority of slaves came to the New World.

West African Kingdoms

Important kingdoms grew strong in the Western Sudan region of Africa where the continent bulges westward into the Atlantic Ocean. Within this region, the three kingdoms of Ghana, Mali

A mask made by the West African Benin tribe in the 1500's.

(or Melle), and Songhai (or Songhay) appeared, flourished, and were finally overthrown. Each of these three kingdoms was well-located along the trading routes that crossed the Sahara. Gold and salt were the two most important products that passed along these routes. Each kingdom that came to power did so by gaining control first over the trade routes and, in turn, over the gold and salt trade. This source of income, plus that from agriculture, crafts, tribute, taxes, and tolls, made Ghana, Mali, and Songhai each rich and powerful, one after the other. These kingdoms developed important traditions that influenced the culture of Africa and entered the heritage of the people. This rich and accomplished background, however, was unknown to the American slave owner.

Ancient and modern territories of Western Africa.

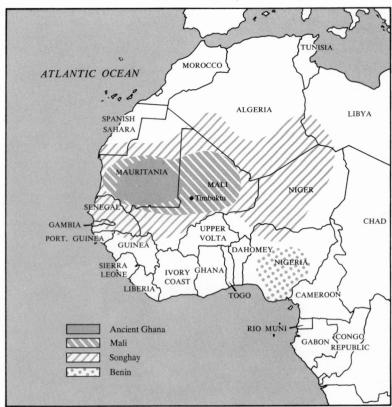

Ghana

Ghana was the first West African kingdom about which we have definite, detailed knowledge. This state occupied a territory different from that of modern Ghana, as you can see in the map. It was already an old and thriving kingdom when first mentioned in the 700's A.D. by an Arab writer. Arab records of that time also mention that forty-four kings had already reigned in Ghana. Tradition says that old Ghana dates back to the 200's.

The kings of Ghana had great power, especially during the 800's, 900's, and 1000's. The strongest, Tenkamenin, ruled in the mid 1000's. Like other kings before him, Tenkamenin was fabulously wealthy. He lived in a beautifully decorated and well-fortified castle. Pictures hung on the walls, pieces of sculpture stood in the rooms, and the windows were worked in designs. During his reign, splendid temples to the gods were built, and magnificent tombs erected in honor of former kings.

The people of the kingdom of Ghana made their living in a number of ways. Some were farmers who cultivated date groves and cared for sheep and cattle, while others traded. Rich deposits of gold in Ghana attracted traders from as far away as Egypt. In exchange for their gold, rubber, and ivory, the merchants of Ghana received textiles, sugar, brass, salt, and wheat from other lands.

Ghana became less powerful after 1076 when a band of new converts to Islam invaded the kingdom. In their desire to establish Islam, these new Moslems brought such great upheaval to the country that Ghana never regained its independent strength.

Mali

Mali, southwest of Ghana, took over the trade routes and reached its greatest power between 1200 and 1400, after the influence of Ghana began to decrease. Many of the people in Mali depended on agriculture for their living. There were also weavers of great skill; rich gold mines supplied much wealth to the nation, and served as a basis for trade.

The most famous ruler of Mali was Mansa Musa (sometimes called Gonga Mussa), who became king in 1307. Strongly under the influence of Islam, Mansa Musa fulfilled the Moslem ambition of making a pilgrimage to Mecca. The splendor of his court was shown on his trip, which he began in 1324. About 60,000 persons accompanied the king. There were soldiers, important officials of the land, royal secretaries, and servants. Five hundred slaves, each carrying a staff of pure gold, walked in a long train. To pay for the expenses of the trip, the king carried gold, twenty-four thousand pounds of it. There was so much gold that it took more than eighty camels with full packs to carry it. In Cairo, on the way to Mecca, Mansa Musa's lavishness caused a mild inflation.

After the 1360's, there were civil wars and the empire of Mali began to break down into smaller tribal kingdoms. During its height, Mali had taken tribute from a subject state to the east, Songhai. In this area was the city of Timbuktu, a center of learning and culture during the reign of Mali. By the mid 1400's, Songhai was able to overrun Mali, take the trade routes, and set itself up as the new kingdom of power in the area.

Songhai

Of the three ancient West African kingdoms, Songhai was the largest and strongest. Its exciting and varied culture was drawn from several sources. From Ghana and Mali came the traditions of farming, commerce, and mining. Like its predecessors, Songhai was blessed with rich gold deposits that attracted traders and trade from nearby and distant European and Asian countries. Because of this foreign trade, there were important contacts with people from different countries, and ideas as well as products were exchanged in this manner.

Education helped the progress of Songhai. In the city of Timbuktu, there was a Moslem university, the University of Sankore, known throughout the civilized world. Negro and Moslem students could study law and surgery there, as well as literature and history. When Negro scholars from the University of Sankore visited the great Moslem university in Cairo, their knowledge amazed the Egyptians. Some of these West African scholars remained in Cairo to teach in the university there.

In 1493, just one year after Columbus discovered America, Songhai's greatest king began his reign. A Moslem, Askia Mohammed brought his kingdom to such a degree of civilization that it compared favorably with any European country of the same period. Askia Mohammed accepted the ideas of many scholars and scientists and established new schools of learning. He reorganized the administrative system that governed the empire, and governors were chosen to rule over the separate provinces of

European map of the 1300's showing Mansa Musa and Timbuktu, as "tenbuch," located at the bottom center.

the kingdom. He improved the system of banking and credit. He introduced laws and legislation and promoted justice. He reorganized the army and extended the boundaries of his empire. He revived the influence of Islam. Timbuktu continued as an intellectual center, and Gao served as the chief commercial center of Songhai. So long as Askia Mohammed was king, the empire prospered.

In 1529 Askia Mohammed's oldest son dethroned him, and Songhai was never so well administered again. Toward the end of the century the Moors, who were Moslems from Morocco, overran Songhai. The culture and civilization of the empire were destroyed. The west coast of Africa soon fell victim to European traders and, eventually, to the slave trade which these traders fostered.

The African Way of Life

The huge continent of Africa, three times as large as the United States, is a land of contrasts. There are great differences in climate, in geographical features, and in groups of people. Even today, the ways in which people live differ in various regions. This was also true in the early history of Africa, though there were some ways of life that were generally followed by all African groups. Similar patterns of organizing government can be traced. There were also similarities in ways of earning a living, in religious observances, and in the development of the arts.

Political Organization

Even the most primitive groups in Africa were organized to an extent where they could try to solve the problems of community living. The simplest type of government was a family grouping, in which all members were related to each other in some manner. The oldest man of the tribe was usually the chieftain, who made the necessary decisions.

A larger tribal group or clan was formed when several families joined together. Clan states were bigger and more powerful than family tribes, and they were more highly organized.

In some areas, several clan villages merged and became a village state. The largest groupings were formed when several village states were joined into a small kingdom. The rulers of the kingdoms had great power. They had regular courts and were surrounded with nobles and advisers. In some kingdoms, there were royal doctors, royal huntsmen, and royal swordbearers. Taxes were collected, and some kingdoms took a regular census of all their people. From the smallest family tribes to the highly organized kingdoms, Africans had worked out a satisfactory way of ruling themselves.

Occupations

Different groups in Africa worked out various ways of making a living. For the most part, they were farmers, raising crops to supply their food. In some areas, land was owned by individual farmers. In other areas, the entire community owned the land. Although individuals worked on the farmland, they made sure that everyone in the village had a share of the crops that were raised. Besides farming, Africans got food by hunting and fishing and in some villages the people were primarily herders. They became skilled in raising and caring for sheep, cattle, goats, and chickens.

Many Africans had skill in making tools and ornaments from metal. They were among the earliest people to use iron successfully, and some historians believe that iron was used in Africa before it was known in Europe and Asia. African blacksmiths of long ago learned to smelt the iron from iron ore and then shape it into tools and objects of beauty. The metal workers of Africa also made their beautifully designed objects from gold, silver, bronze, and copper.

Other products that showed the skill and talent of African craftsmen were baskets, woven cloth, glazed pottery, wood carvings, and rugs. In some regions, whole villages would specialize in making one product. Craftsmen of one village, for example, excelled in making weapons and tools, while the people in another wove fine cloth. Because of this specialization, trading developed between the tribes and village states. In this manner, there was a constant give and take of ideas and products among the village states of Africa.

Religion

Religious beliefs and customs differed in the various parts of Africa, but most of the people believed that there was one all-powerful god who had created the world and all its creatures. They believed, also, that the spirits of men lived after death. These spirits continued to make their homes on earth, close to the living members of their families. As we have seen, family life was very important to Africans, and part of their religion was based on the worship of the spirits of their ancestors. They felt that the spirits of their forefathers watched over and protected them, and in return they worshiped these spirits, as well as the places where they thought the spirits lived.

The priest was an important member of every tribe and village. He alone had the special power to communicate with the spirits and to conduct the ceremonies of religious worship.

The Arts

Thoughts and feelings may be experienced but never communicated or they may also be expressed through art, music, and literature. These forms of creative expression, called the arts, were definitely a part of the early African way of life.

Arts and Crafts.   The art work of Africa is highly original and is done with skill. Sometimes early African art was an expression of a religious feeling. The artist tried to create an image of one of the spirits which were a part of his world. Strange carvings were the result, for the spirit world was full of mystery. Carving was an important art form and artists worked with the materials at hand: ivory, wood, and stone. Today early African carving occupies a place of honor in the art world and is considered one of the sources of inspiration for modern art.

A leopard from the Benin bronze workers, 1600's.

Other crafts that showed a high degree of skill were also developed by talented artisans. Pottery was covered with original designs and then glazed. Skill in weaving resulted in baskets, cloth, tapestries, and mats. Jewelry was made from gold and silver, and vases and other ornaments were fashioned from bronze and brass. The designs with which these objects were decorated showed the Africans' desire to make everyday objects beautiful as well as useful.

Many notable examples of African art come from two Yoruba tribes, the Ife and the Benin. These tribes lived in the forest region of western Africa in what is now Nigeria. The first people to come to these forests were reported to have started from Mecca, in Arabia, but very little is known about them before 1000 A.D. Because of similarities in art styles, it is believed that the Ife during the years 1200 B.C. and 200 A.D. were under considerable influence from a group of farming people living on the plains nearby. At any rate, the art of the Ife, especially work done in bronze, eventually influenced that of the Benin tribe, which had settled farther south, on the Niger River.

Chieftain's carved wooden chair, from Cameroun.

Music. The music often associated with Africa is that of the tom-tom. Tom-toms were used to accompany dances, but singing was important, too. There were several types of songs to fit different occasions: lullabies, dance songs, work songs, and religious songs. One style of singing has been described as the call and response. A solo voice would sing the "call," and a chorus would join in the "response."

Musicians played on instruments designed and constructed in Africa. Some of the different types of instruments that were used by Africans were flutes, violins, harps, guitars, zithers, xylophones, trumpets, and bugles.

Literature. The many different languages of Africa made communication among the various villages difficult. In southern Africa alone, for example, there were at least 182 different Bantu languages. Few of the languages were written; people could communicate with each other only by the spoken word. Stories could not be read but only heard, and so oral literature became part of the lives of the people of Africa. Fathers repeated fables to their sons, and storytellers went from village to village. In these ways, stories and myths were handed down to each generation.

Many different types of stories and poems came from Africa. Some were myths in which strange and unusual happenings were explained. There were tales of the spirit world and moral tales that taught a lesson. Epic poems described acts of courage; and love songs, comic stories, and funeral recitations were repeated on the appropriate occasion. The practical wisdom of the people is shown in proverbs like these:

"The lack of knowledge is darker than night."

"Not to know is bad; not to wish to know is worse."

"The dawn does not come twice to wake a man." [1]

---

[1] Carter Woodson, *The Negro in Our History,* edited by C. H. Wesley (Washington, D.C.: The Associated Publishers, Inc., 1959).

Exploration and Colonization

Negroes have taken an active part in every period of American history. They came with the Spanish explorers who searched the New World for spices and wealth. They shared the dangers and the thrill of new discoveries with leaders of exploring parties.

Later, they were brought in chains from their native lands to live in the colonies. They struggled, as did other colonists, to build settlements in a new country. Their efforts in clearing the land and raising crops were important contributions to colonial life.

Period of Exploration

Many of the Spanish explorers who came to the New World brought Negroes with them, as slaves or servants. Other Negroes came as free men, and some held important positions. It is possible that Alonzo Pietro (also called Pedro Alonso Niño), the captain of one of Columbus' three ships, the *Niña,* was a Negro. He is referred to as a man of color, but this need not mean specifically a Negro.

Free Negroes definitely accompanied other explorers. They were with Coronado, DeSoto, and Pizarro. In 1513, Balboa led an

27

One version of the landing of the Jamestown Negroes.

expedition across the Isthmus of Panama and became the first European to see the Pacific Ocean. Among his men were thirty Negroes, one of whom was named Nuflo de Olano.

Negroes with Cortez

Another famous Spanish explorer, Hernando Cortez, heard of a land that was rich in gold and silver, located west of the island of Cuba. In 1519, Cortez set out for Mexico with an army of five hundred men, among whom were some Negroes. Besides his army of Spaniards and Negroes, there were about three hundred Indians from the New World who joined his forces. Cortez and his followers were successful in conquering the Aztec Indians in the rich land of Mexico. Great amounts of Mexican gold and silver were sent back to Spain. Another interesting accomplishment of Cortez and his men is not so well known. The Spaniards brought both rice and wheat into Mexico for the first time. Negro laborers planted grains of wheat in Mexico and later harvested the first wheat crop grown on the continent of North America.

Estevan

One of the most interesting of the Negro explorers was Estevan or Estevanico, whose name meant Stephen or Little Stephen in Spanish. Born in Morocco, Estevan was a servant, and sailed with five or six hundred men from Spain in 1527 to look for riches and to explore the New World. The expedition was headed by Panfilo de Narvaez, who landed first in the West Indies. Some of the party stayed there, and only about half of the group was still together when the expedition landed on the Florida coast. Gradually the group was reduced to only four men, including Estevan. Lack of food, illness, and harassment by the Indians had killed all but these four men as the group wandered along the Gulf coast toward what is now Texas. Finally, Estevan, Cabeza de Vaca, and two others were captured by a band of Indians near Texas. The Indians made the four men work for them as traders, slaves, and amateur doctors. The tribe came to respect their power to heal, since the four men knew more about medicine than the

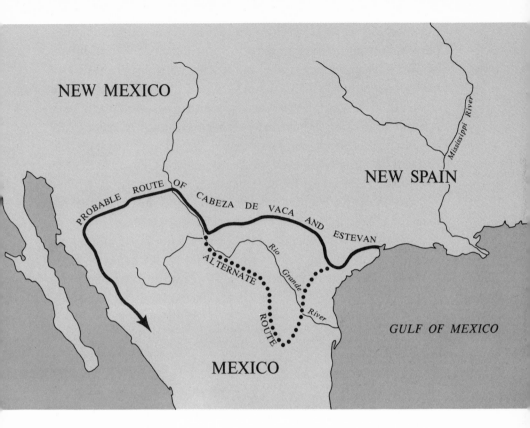

Route of Cabeza de Vaca and Estevan to Mexico City.

Indians. While living with this tribe, Estevan picked up a detailed knowledge of the land and of Indian languages. All four men escaped in 1534 and began a trek west and south, reaching the Spanish settlement of Mexico City ten months later.

Cabeza de Vaca excited the viceroy of New Spain in Mexico City by telling him the stories and Indian legends he and the three other men had heard on the way from the Texas territory. These were stories of the Seven Cities of Cibola, probably seven separate pueblo cities of the Zuñi Indians in the territory that is now New Mexico. The legend told of cities all ruled by one man and built of fine stone and decorated with turquoise. The viceroy somehow obtained Estevan who was to serve as the guide for an exploring party that would return north to look for the cities. Friar Marcus of Nice headed the expedition, but it was guided by Estevan. The group started out in 1539. Estevan was sent ahead of the party as an advance scout, and it was agreed that he would send back a wooden cross to indicate any riches he found. A small cross would mean a small discovery and a large cross, much riches. Estevan apparently reached or heard talk of Cibola, itself, the first of the Zuñi cities. He sent back a cross as large as a man. But before his party could join him, he was captured by the Indians of Cibola and killed.

Estevan is to be remembered for leading the first explorations into the deserts of the Southwest, opening up the exploration of the land that was later to become New Mexico and Arizona.

Negroes in the English Colonies

Unlike the Spanish, the English explorers brought no Negroes with them on their expeditions to the New World. No Negroes were present in the first English colonies in North America, neither in the lost colony of Sir Walter Raleigh, nor in the little settlement at Jamestown. It was twelve years after the founding of Jamestown that Negroes first made an appearance there. In 1619, a Dutch ship, headed for the West Indies, dropped anchor, instead, in Jamestown harbor with twenty Africans on board. The captain was short of food and other provisions, and he wanted to exchange the Negroes for supplies. He traded them not as slaves but as indentured workers, which meant that they had to work for a few years without pay. These twenty Negroes became the first settlers from Africa to make their homes in an English colony. Five years later, in 1624, little William Tucker was born. He was the first Negro child to be born in what was to become the United States.

These first settlers from Africa, like the later ones, did not come voluntarily. They were captured and brought against their will to the New World. The Spanish had discovered years before that it took hard work to establish colonies in a new land. There was a constant shortage of workers. Since the early 1500's, Spanish ships had carried captives from Africa to work as slaves in the new Spanish colonies. This procedure was gradually imitated by other European nations, especially the English and the Dutch.

From Servitude to Slavery

At first the Africans in the English settlements were not slaves. They worked as indentured servants in the same way as did some of the white colonists from Europe. An indentured servant worked for his master for a certain period of time, usually from five to seven years. During the time of his indenture, or service, he received no wages for his work. Instead, he was supplied with certain necessities, such as food, shelter, and clothing. At the end of his period of indenture, he was free. He could work for wages; he could buy his own land; he could move freely from place to place. In this manner, the first Negroes served their indenture and then took their place in the community as free colonists. They built their own homes, and a few became the masters of other indentured servants. For a while, Negroes in the colonies had much the same opportunities as other settlers.

As the new settlements became more firmly established, survival was no longer the main concern of the colonists. They looked for ways to make money and used the fertile soil to produce tobacco and cotton for sale in Europe. Huge farms were planted, and many workers were needed. Planters needed a cheap supply of labor. At first, indentured servants were used to cultivate the fields, but their term of service was short. Sometimes indentured workers escaped and succeeded in reaching a different settlement before their indenture had been completed. The planters tried for a time to force the Indians to work in the fields. This plan was not successful. Many Indians knew the territory so well that they easily escaped and returned to the forests. Others became sick and died. Indian labor seemed to be more trouble than it was worth to the planters. They found Negroes to be effective workers and so conditions for the Negroes became harsher. Negro indentured laborers, for example, had to work for longer periods of time than European servants in order to gain their freedom. By the 1650's, Negroes had little chance of actually earning their freedom in the English colonies. Most of the Africans brought to the colonies came to be regarded as servants for life. Even though they were called indentured servants, their period of indenture lasted a lifetime. Then in the 1660's, Maryland and Virginia passed laws making slavery legal within those colonies. Other colonies followed this example. In time, slavery became a legal institution in most of the colonies and was recognized by all of them.

Slavery existed legally in our country from the 1660's until 1865. It became strongest in the South, where large plantations were developed to grow cotton and tobacco. Even when slavery was at its height, the majority of southerners did not own slaves. Many individuals had small farms, and they and their families did all the necessary work of raising crops. Slavery was at its peak during the 1850's and in 1860 about one in every twenty southerners owned slaves. There were about eight million white southerners and about 384,000 slaveholders.

The Middle Passage

With the growth of slavery in the colonies came the demand for more and more slaves. Planters were willing to pay high prices for healthy workers, and the slave trade flourished.

New England shipowners who took part in the slave trade established a three-way route. Loaded with manufactured goods, ships left New England and sailed to the west coast of Africa. In Africa, the manufactured products were traded for slaves. With the cargo of slaves, the ships again crossed the Atlantic to the West Indies. There, many of the slaves were sold, and the empty ships were reloaded with molasses. From the West Indies, the ships returned to New England, where they delivered the molasses and picked up manufactured goods.

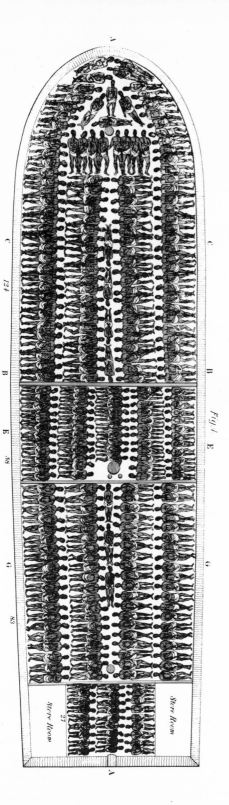

*Loading plan
for the lower deck
of a British slave ship.
The drawing shows
450 slaves
in an area measuring
100 feet by 25 feet.*

The second part of the route, from Africa to the West Indies, was often called the Middle Passage. Conditions on the over-crowded slave ships were so frightful that the trip was like a night-mare. Every available space was used to pack in the greatest pos-sible number of slaves. Chained together by two's, the unhappy captives had just enough space to lie down. Wedged beneath the upper deck in the hold of the ship, the future slaves spent most of the fifty-day voyage without light or fresh air. Disease was common, and many of the captives died before reaching the New World. On an average voyage, death came to approximately one slave out of every eight. Some slave ships reported even greater losses.

Slavery on the Plantations

In the hold of the slave ship, the captured African ceased being considered a person. He became a piece of property that would be sold for a certain sum of money, and that is how he was re-garded by the man who bought him at the slave auction.

New arrivals from Africa needed training in their future duties. During the breaking-in period, they were placed for instruction in the care of experienced slaves. Their learning was not volun-tary, but forced. They had to speak in English, rather than in their native dialects. Other new ideas and habits were forced upon them. The demands of their harsh new life made it impossible for the new slaves to practice their African customs. Unlike the Eng-lish, who transferred many of their traditions to the New World, the African slave had to abandon his. In time, he realized what slavery meant. He learned that no matter how hard or how well he worked, he could not earn his freedom unless his master granted him permission to do so. He would never be allowed to own property or to travel about from place to place without per-mission from his master. In most cases, he would not even be permitted to learn to read and write. He would be in bondage for his entire life.

The master had complete control over the life of his "property." He could buy or sell his slaves, or give them away as he saw fit.

BY

HEWLETT & BRIGHT.

SALE OF

VALUABLE SLAVES,

(On account of departure)

The Owner of the following named and valuable Slaves, being on the eve of departure for Europe, will cause the same to be offered for sale, at the NEW EXCHANGE, corner of St. Louis and Chartres streets, on *Saturday,* May 16, at Twelve o'Clock, *viz.*

1. SARAH, a mulatress, aged 45 years, a good cook and accustomed to house work in general, is an excellent and faithful nurse for sick persons, and in every respect a first rate character.

2. DENNIS, her son, a mulatto, aged 24 years, a first rate cook and steward for a vessel, having been in that capacity for many years on board one of the Mobile packets; is strictly honest, temperate, and a first rate subject.

3. CHOLE, a mulatress, aged 36 years, she is, without execption, one of the most competent servants in the country, a first rate washer and ironer, does up lace, a good cook, and for a bachelor who wishes a house-keeper she would be invaluable; she is also a good ladies' maid, having travelled to the North in that capacity.

4. FANNY, her daughter, a mulatress, aged 16 years, speaks French and English, is a superior hair-dresser, (pupil of Guilliac,) a good seamstress and ladies' maid, is smart, intelligent, and a first rate character.

5. DANDRIDGE, a mulatoo, aged 26 years, a first rate dining-room servant, a good painter and rough carpenter, and has but few equals for honesty and sobriety.

6. NANCY, his wife, aged about 24 years, a confidential house servant, good seamstress, mantuamaker and tailoress, a good cook, washer and ironer, etc.

7. MARY ANN, her child, a creole, aged 7 years, speaks French and English, is smart, active and intelligent.

8. FANNY or FRANCES, a mulatress, aged 22 years, is a first rate washer and ironer, good cook and house servant, and has an excellent character.

9. EMMA, an orphan, aged 10 or 11 years, speaks French and English, has been in the country 7 years, has been accustomed to waiting on table, sewing etc.; is intelligent and active.

10. FRANK, a mulatto, aged about 32 years speaks French and English, is a first rate hostler and coachman, understands perfectly well the management of horses, and is, in every respect, a first rate character, with the exception that he will occasionally drink, though not an habitual drunkard.

All the above named Slaves are acclimated and excellent subjects; they were purchased by their present vendor many years ago, and will, therefore, be severally warranted against all vices and maladies prescribed by law, save and except FRANK, who is fully guaranteed in every other respect but the one above mentioned.

TERMS:—One-half Cash, and the other half in notes at Six months, drawn and endorsed to the satisfaction of the Vendor, with special mortgage on the Slaves until final payment. The Acts of Sale to be passed before WILLIAM BOSWELL, *Notary Public,* at the expense of the Purchaser.

New-Orleans, May 13, 1835.

PRINTED BY BENJAMIN LEVY.

Advertisement for the sale of slaves.

He could separate members of the slave family, selling one person away from the rest of the family. He could punish or reward the slaves according to his wishes. Each slave owner, then, had a direct influence over the conditions under which the slave worked. If the master was kind, being a slave was difficult; but if he was harsh, it was a dreary life, almost impossible to endure.

The plantation system of agriculture spread throughout Virginia, the Carolinas, and Maryland, although small farms continued to exist. Farmers with small land holdings often owned no more than three to five slaves. On these small farms, master and slaves worked side by side in the fields. More prosperous planters owned as many as ten to thirty slaves, while owners of the largest plantations sometimes had hundreds. The planter and his family lived in a large, beautifully furnished house. Surrounding the big house were many outbuildings—a barn, stable, carriage house, smoke house, hen house, kitchen, wash room, black-

The life of the field slave included hoeing.

smith shop, and carpenter shed. The slave cabins were located close to the big house, too. Large tobacco sheds, where the important money crop of the colonists was carefully cured and prepared for market, stood in the fields.

In each of the buildings and in the fields, slaves provided the labor. The slaves of larger plantations were divided roughly into two groups. The field hands did the heavy work of clearing and cultivating the land and caring for the crops. At sunrise their work started, and it continued through the day until dusk. One old slave, who had spent most of his life working as a field hand, said, "The fields stretched from one end of the earth to the other!" [1]

The house slaves, who kept the big house running efficiently, were chosen and trained with care. They were the cooks and laundresses, maids and butlers, and the nurses for the children. The slaves who worked in the big house were usually better fed than the field hands, for they got their meals from the kitchen, close at hand. Certainly, their clothing was finer than the coarse, strong working clothes that were given to the field hands twice every year. The house slaves were often given the cast-off clothing of the planter's family. No one seemed to think it strange that a maid in a big house would eventually wear a fine dress that had been made in England. Because they were so closely associated with the planter's family, the house servants often felt a loyalty and affection for members of the family. They had the opportunity, also, to copy the speech and manners of the family they served and some of the children of house servants were given the chance to learn to read.

Since large plantations were usually located far from villages and farms, much of the necessary equipment had to be made on the plantation. Skilled slaves worked as carpenters, brickmakers, coopers, blacksmiths, and butchers. Negro craftsmanship produced the beautiful wrought-iron balustrades that can still be seen on old homes in Charleston and New Orleans. Skilled slaves

[1] Lerone Bennett, *Before the Mayflower* (Chicago: Johnson Publishing Company, Inc., 1962), p. 87.

were considered more valuable than field hands. There were some
slave owners who allowed their skilled slaves to leave the plantation and hire themselves out as workers for wages. From his
wages, the slave would pay his master a certain sum of money.
Any money that he earned beyond that sum would be his to
keep. Through hard work, a few slaves were able to earn enough
money to buy their freedom, with the permission of their owners.

Slaves fashioned balustrades for these New Orleans homes.

The Revolutionary War Era

During the years from 1607 to 1770, English settlements in the New World grew from one weak village at Jamestown to thirteen well-established colonies. Settlers had proved they could do more than merely survive in the wilderness. They had built towns where none had existed before. They had become successful businessmen, selling products of farm, forest, and sea. Colonial ships loaded with American products were a familiar sight in the harbors of England and the West Indies. The settlers were taking an active part in the government of their colonies. In the House of Burgesses in Virginia and the town meetings in New England, colonists shared in the making of laws. They had developed self-confidence and a strong feeling of independence.

During these years of growth, the number of Negroes living in the colonies was increasing, too. By 1770, there were more than 350,000 Negroes. Most of them were slaves, owned by slaveholders in both the northern and southern colonies. Some of the Negroes were free. The census of 1790 gave their number as 59,000. See Appendix II, at the back of the book, for further figures. In the South, the free Negroes lived on small farms or in towns where they worked as skilled craftsmen. Free Negroes in the northern colonies lived in cities where they had a better chance to earn a living.

How did they become free? Some were born free, the descendants of the first groups of indentured servants who had worked
out their terms of service. Others had saved money and had bought
their freedom, and still others had been freed by their masters.
A few were runaways who had escaped to freedom. The Negro
freemen were caught up in the spirit of independence that was
growing in the colonies. What lay ahead for them?

The Revolutionary War

In the 1760's, Great Britain passed a series of laws that angered
the colonies. In 1763, a British army was stationed in the colonies, and the Americans had to pay for its support with new taxes.
Then followed the Navigation Acts that placed limits on colonial
shipping. Next came the hated Stamp Act, which caused the colonists to protest, "Taxation without representation is tyranny!"
Each new law the British passed made the colonists more resent-
ful and added to their desire for independence. Children echoed
the displeasure of their elders. When they saw the British officers
with their red coats, they would yell, "Lobsterback!" and then
run and hide.

Crispus Attucks and the Boston Massacre

It was in Boston on March 5, 1770, that a small incident got
out of control. Here the first American patriots died for freedom,
and one of those patriots was a Negro. It started with a simple
act. A boy threw a snowball at a British sentry. An uproar followed, and soon there was a mob made up of British soldiers
armed with rifles and American colonists holding stones and
sticks. Among the angry colonists was Crispus Attucks, a tall
Negro sailor who had escaped from slavery about twenty years
before this time. He was well known around the docks of lower
Boston. Shouting their defiance at the British soldiers, Attucks
and the colonists threw stones and sticks. The British troops re-
taliated. Under orders, they fired into the angry crowd. There

was a sudden sound of gunfire, and Crispus Attucks and two others lay dead on King Street. Two other Americans died later from wounds suffered that day. In all, five died.

This act, called the Boston Massacre, aroused the fury of the colonists. It made them more determined than ever to stand up for their rights. Elaborate funeral services were held in Faneuil Hall for Attucks and his companions. The following description of the funeral procession, which fails to mention Patrick Carr, the fifth victim, was printed in a Boston newspaper, *The Gazette and Country Journal:*

Last Thursday, agreeable to a general Request of the Inhabitants, and by the Consent of Parents and Friends, were carried to their Grave in Succession, the Bodies of Samuel Gray, Samuel Maverick, James Caldwell, and Crispus Attucks, the unhappy Victims who fell in the bloody Massacre of the Monday Evening preceding!

On this Occasion most of the Shops in Town were shut, all the Bells were ordered to toll a solemn Peal, as were also in the neighboring Towns of Charlestown, Roxbury, &. The Procession began to move between the Hours of 4 and 5 in the Afternoon; two of the unfortunate Sufferers, viz. James Caldwell and Crispus Attucks, who were Strangers, borne from Faneuil-Hall, attended by a numerous Train of Persons of all Ranks; and the other two, viz. Mr. Samuel Gray, from the House of Mr. Benjamin Gray (his brother) on the North-side of the Exchange, and Mr. Maverick, from the House of his distressed Mother, Mrs. Mary Maverick, in Union-Street, each followed by their respective Relations and Friends. The several Hearses forming a Junction in King-Street, the Theater of that inhuman tragedy! proceded from thence thro' Main-Street, lengthened by an immense Concourse of People, so numerous as to be obliged to follow in Ranks of Six and brought up by a long Train of Carriages belonging to the principal Gentry of the Town. The Bodies were deposited in one Vault in the middle Burying-ground: The aggravated Circumstances of their Death, the Distress and Sorrow visible in every Countenance, together with the peculiar Solemnity with which the whole Funeral was conducted, surpasses Description.[1]

---

[1] Langston Hughes and Milton Meltzer, *A Pictorial History of the Negro in America* (New York: Crown Publishers, Inc., 1963), p. 57.

An over-orderly version of Crispus Attucks' death in Boston.

In 1888, a tall monument was erected in honor of the five victims of the Boston Massacre. Located in the Boston Common, the monument lists the names of the patriots. It also contains the following words written by John Adams about the Boston Massacre, "On that night, the foundation of American independence was laid."

Negroes in the Revolutionary War

The stirring words of the Declaration of Independence expressed the colonists' longing for liberty and the rights of man. Because men were willing to struggle and fight for their freedom, the colonists dared to revolt against Great Britain. The Revolutionary War began with the battles of Lexington and Concord in 1775. Eight years later in 1783, the final peace treaty was signed by both Great Britain and an independent nation, the United States of America.

Before the end of the war, both the British and Continental Armies had promised freedom to American slaves who would join their ranks. Negroes served with each army, seeking a chance to earn their freedom.

Negroes in the British Army. Faced with a shortage of manpower, the British Commander-in-Chief promised freedom to American slaves in exchange for their service in his army. In the South, thousands of slaves escaped from their masters and joined the British forces. Used largely as laborers, rather than fighters, the majority of the ex-slaves worked as carpenters, teamsters, blacksmiths, and axmen. Because of their knowledge of the territory, others served well as guides and spies. A few Negroes were given arms and fought as soldiers with the British Army.

After the war, the Americans were anxious to reclaim the slaves who had fought with the British. The British refused to give them up, pointing out that freedom had been promised to these men. When the British armed forces sailed away from America, their ships carried about 14,000 Negroes. Many of them settled in Canada or in the British West Indies, beyond the reach of American slavery.

Negroes with the Continental Army. The colonial forces, too, were strengthened by freedom-seeking Negroes. Negro soldiers, at first not welcomed as recruits, stood out as heroes because of their courage.

Peter Salem stood fast with other patriots at Lexington and Concord. He fought also in the Battle of Bunker Hill, and it is sometimes said that his was the very shot that killed Major Pitcairn, one of the British officers. Another soldier, Salem Poor, fought so bravely in this same battle that he was later praised by fourteen officers. They said he "behaved like an experienced officer, as well as an excellent soldier." [2] Besides the two soldiers named Salem, there was Prince Whipple who rode in the boat with General George Washington when the American troops crossed the icy Delaware River on Christmas Day in 1776. They surprised the British at Trenton, New Jersey, and took one thousand prisoners of war on the following day. Austin Dabney was another Negro who served in the Continental Army. He entered the army as a slave and was fighting for his own freedom and that of his country. He not only got his freedom but, as a reward for bravery, he got a tract of land in Georgia and a pension from the United States government.

As the Revolutionary War progressed, all the soldiers faced hardships and real suffering. A shortage of food and other supplies added to their discomfort. There was a crucial lack of manpower. The British Commander-in-Chief had already made his offer to the Negroes and in December 1775 General George Washington, who had been reluctant to enlist Negroes, called for all Negro freemen to come to the defense of their country and join the army. By 1778, the slaves themselves were also recruited into the Continental Army and freedom was promised to those

[2] Benjamin Quarles, *The Negro in the American Revolution* (Chapel Hill, North Carolina: University of North Carolina Press), 1961, p. 11.

who answered the call to arms. Negro troops, fighting side by side
with other soldiers, took part in most of the important battles,
and the officers who commanded them praised their courage. By
the end of the war, at least five thousand Negroes had served in
the Continental Army. Some historians believe that even a greater
number of Negroes had served. They point out that, because careful records were not kept in those early days, an accurate count
is difficult to make, but it is clear that thousands of Negroes shared
with other patriots in the dangers and glory of bringing forth a
new nation.

The Spirit of Freedom

In the troubled days before the Revolutionary War, the colonists had become greatly concerned with freedom. Their wish for
independence from Great Britain caused them to think carefully
about their rights and about the rights of all men. During these
times when the word *freedom* was on everyone's tongue, individuals and organizations began to speak out against slavery.

Some colonial leaders expressed their personal disapproval of
slavery. Thomas Jefferson and General Lafayette both stated
publicly that slavery was evil. Leaders from both the North and
the South opposed slavery at this time. Benjamin Franklin from
Pennsylvania expressed his opposition to slavery, as did the south-
erner Patrick Henry. Still other leaders did more than speak out
against slavery; they showed their disapproval by their actions.
Even a foreign visitor tried to help the slaves. This was Thaddeus
Kosciusko, the Polish patriot who served in the Revolutionary
War. He arranged that the money he had earned in America be
used for two purposes—first, to buy the freedom of slaves and
second, to educate them to become useful citizens. Benjamin
Franklin acted, too. For years, he served as the chairman of an
antislavery society in Philadelphia. The purposes of this organization were to work for the freedom of slaves and to prepare the
newly freed slaves for citizenship. Other leaders who acted upon
their convictions were George Washington and Thomas Jefferson.
Upon their deaths, both men freed all their slaves.

A Negro soldier can be seen fighting at Bunker Hill.

In the middle and late 1700's, organizations that opposed slavery were formed. The Quakers felt that their religious beliefs required them to try to bring an end to slavery. Other church groups also became interested in this work, particularly the Methodists and Baptists. They helped to organize antislavery societies that tried to free individuals whenever possible and worked to end slavery wherever it existed in the country. For a while, their efforts were rewarding.

After the Revolutionary War, a great interest in the ideas of freedom continued. The colonists had gained their freedom from Great Britain, but they saw within their new, free nation a group of people who had no personal freedom. This was a troubling thought to many, especially when they remembered the courage of the Negro soldiers in the Revolutionary War. Some of the new states began, one by one, to write provisions against slavery into their state constitutions. Vermont, in 1777, was the first state to forbid slavery within its borders. New Hampshire, Pennsylvania, Connecticut, Rhode Island, Massachusetts, and New York had all made some provisions against slavery by 1800. Other states were following their examples.

Still another step against slavery was taken by the United States Congress. One result of the Revolutionary War had been the gaining of additional lands by the new nation. At the close of the war, Great Britain agreed to give to the United States all the territory south of the Great Lakes and east of the Mississippi River. The northwestern part of this vast region was called the Northwest Territory. Before settlers could move into this new part of the United States, however, laws had to be established. In 1787, Congress passed the Northwest Ordinance, an important law which provided for the government of that territory. One part of the Northwest Ordinance stated that slavery was forbidden within the Northwest Territory. By this action, it seemed that slavery would not reach into new territories of the United States.

Postponement of Freedom for All

While steps were being made toward freedom for the Negro, other events which slowed progress were taking place. After the Revolutionary War, the new nation faced many problems. How would the country be governed? How could the former colonies be united into one strong country and still, as states, keep some of their rights? How could money be raised to meet the expenses of running a country? How could the weak infant nation protect its rights against the other strong countries of the world? These were questions that had to be solved immediately if the United States was to survive as a nation. The problem of slavery or freedom for the Negroes seemed to be less crucial and was, therefore, postponed.

Constitutional Convention

The leaders of the United States first worked out a plan of government for the new country. A meeting, the Constitutional Convention, was held in Philadelphia in 1787. Delegates to the convention had the task of writing the Constitution, a document that would define the powers of the new government. The Constitution would state how taxes would be raised, how laws for the country would be made, how the President and representatives from each state would be chosen. In working out some of these problems, delegates from various states sometimes disagreed. Two of the points of disagreement were directly concerned with slavery. They were the problems of raising taxes and of choosing representatives.

The Constitutional Convention decided that the laws for the nation would be made by Congress, a group of men elected from each state. Congress, itself, would be made up of two groups or houses. To one, the Senate, each state would send two representatives. Whether a state was large or small was unimportant; it would send the same number of representatives as every other state. Membership in the other house, the House of Representatives, was different. The number of its members would depend on the population of the state. A state with many people, like Pennsylvania, would elect more members to the House of Representatives than would a small state, like Maryland.

It was also decided that each state would pay taxes to support the national government. The amount of taxes paid by any state would depend on its population. The larger states with greater populations would pay more taxes than smaller states.

The discussion of population raised an interesting question in the Constitutional Convention. Would slaves be counted as property or as people? Since each state wanted as many members in the House of Representatives as possible, a large population was an advantage. But since no state wanted to pay more taxes than it had to, a small population was desirable. The farming states of the South had the greatest number of slaves, and they wanted to count them in two different ways. When they were deciding how many members to send to the House of Representatives, they wanted to count slaves as people, part of their total population. But when they were deciding the amount of their taxes, they wanted to count the slaves as property, not population. Other states with small numbers of slaves would not agree with these ways of counting population. Finally, an agreement, or compromise, was reached. The compromise stated that three slaves out of every five should be counted as population when deciding both the number of representatives and the amount of taxation. In addition, the Constitution stated that after twenty years no more slaves could be brought in from Africa. The problem of slavery would be faced, but in the future.

Important Inventions

Other events which took place in the 1790's had a far-reaching influence on the whole question of slavery. Machines, which did the work of many men, brought rapid changes into the lives of people. The machines introduced by two men, Samuel Slater and Eli Whitney, were particularly important in making the system of slavery stronger in our country.

A worker guides cotton bolls through a gin, separating seeds.

Power Spinning Machine and Loom. Samuel Slater had lived in England and had worked in textile factories there before he came to America. He had worked with machines that spun thread and then wove the thread into cloth. He had seen for himself how much more rapidly and evenly machines could do this work than men could, working by hand. When Slater came to America, he settled in Rhode Island. Finding no machines to do the work of spinning and weaving, he set to work and built from memory a spinning machine and a power loom. His machines were copied, and many were built in the New England states. Cloth could be made rapidly with machinery, and the New England factories needed a large supply of cotton from which to make it.

The Cotton Gin. The southern states had plenty of land and a climate perfect for the growing of cotton, but the southern plant-

ers faced a problem in raising such large amounts of cotton for the factories in New England. Separating the cotton seeds from the fiber was a slow, painstaking job.

In 1793, Eli Whitney developed his cotton gin, and this gin solved the problem of removing cotton seeds rapidly. The idea came to him as he saw Negro slaves using homemade mechanical methods for separating cotton fiber from the seeds. By using Whitney's cotton gin, planters were able to prepare greater amounts of cotton for factory use. More land was used in the growing of cotton, which became the main money-producing crop of the South. Although figures differ for the increase in cotton production after the invention of the cotton gin, it would be safe to estimate that thirty years after the gin, the South produced at least seventy-five times as much cotton as it had before. Planters bought new land upon which to raise cotton and, in time, the cotton belt reached as far west as the Mississippi River. When plantations became larger, many slaves were needed to clear the land and cultivate the crop. The slave trade with Africa flourished, and the whole system of slavery became more firmly established.

Outstanding Negroes

Besides the soldiers who had served so well in the Revolutionary War, there were other Negroes who contributed to the history of the United States. Some of them had once been slaves who had managed to gain their freedom. All of them had succeeded in making the most of their limited chances of getting an education. Each one became outstanding in spite of the handicap of racial prejudice, which made their efforts more difficult.

Benjamin Banneker. This inventor, surveyor, mathematician, and astronomer was born of free parents in the colony of Maryland in 1731. His hard-working parents owned their tobacco farm and were highly respected in the community.

Young Banneker's grandmother started the boy's education. She taught him how to read, using the Bible as a text. When a Quaker schoolmaster opened a school in the community, Benjamin became an eager pupil. He was especially interested in mathematics, and on more than one occasion he noticed mistakes in the schoolbooks that were used. After he left school, he continued his friendship with the Quaker schoolmaster and often borrowed books from his friend's collection.

When he was a young man, he became interested in making an instrument to show time. At first, he made plans for a sundial. This didn't satisfy him, however, for he wanted to show the time even when the sun was not shining. Then fate stepped in. He was given a watch by a friend, and his interest became feverish. His Quaker friend showed him a picture of a clock and explained how some clocks even struck the hour. Benjamin Banneker wondered how this was done. He borrowed books on higher mathematics and geometric theory and pored over them. Then he started to experiment. For a year, for two years, for three, he carefully carved from wood the inner workings of a clock. His efforts were finally successful, for the finished clock kept accurate time and struck the hours. People for miles around came to look at the clock and marvel. It was the first clock that many had ever seen. This clock was the first to be made in Maryland, and perhaps the first striking clock made in all the American colonies.

Benjamin Banneker continued his program of reading and self-education. From a borrowed book, he developed an interest in the study of stars, or astronomy. He read deeply and made his own observations at night. After successfully working out a prediction of solar eclipses, he thought of an idea for still another project. Benjamin Banneker wrote an almanac and every year from 1791 to 1802 a new Banneker Almanac made its appearance. His fame as a scholar went far beyond his Maryland homeland.

By this time, the colonies had thrown off the rule of Great Britain and had become one nation, struggling to become united and strong. The new country needed, among other things, a capital city where all the governmental offices would be located. It must be a beautiful city, worthy of a great nation. Careful plans would be made before any building was started. For this project, the talents of some of the finest surveyors, geographers, and scholars were used. Among them was Benjamin Banneker. He was appointed by President Thomas Jefferson to work with other intelligent and trustworthy men in helping the French engineer Pierre L'Enfant prepare the plans for Washington, D.C. His ability and hard work won the respect of all who were helping with the same project.

Phillis Wheatley.   Does it seem strange that a slave girl in Boston would be one of the first women poets of America? Phillis Wheatley was a slave and she wrote poems that were read as far away as London, England.

Born in Africa, Phillis was captured and sent to America when she was only about eight years old. She reached the city of Boston in 1761. Although she was thin and frail-looking, her eyes were alert. It was her eyes that attracted the attention of John Wheatley, who was looking for a girl to serve as his wife's maid. He bought the child and gave her the family name of Wheatley, as was often the custom of slaveholders.

The little girl from Africa soon learned to speak the English language. She responded eagerly to the lessons given by Mary, the Wheatley daughter. Soon she was reading every book she could find and was doing some writing of her own.

Phillis Wheatley was never strong. When she was about twenty years old, her health became worse. The Wheatleys gave her freedom to her and took her to London, hoping that she would become stronger. While she was in London, her first book, *Poems on Various Subjects,* was published in 1773.

When she returned to Boston, she was a well-known poet. She wrote a poem honoring George Washington, who had been appointed as Commander-in-Chief of the American Army. From him she received a gracious letter of thanks. During these years problems came into Phillis Wheatley's life. Mrs. Wheatley, who had always been a friend rather than a mistress, died. Phillis had an unfortunate marriage. She lived through the heartbreaking experience of seeing two of her children die of disease. She herself

Phillis Wheatley

struggled against poverty. Finally, overwork and poor health were too much for the frail poet. In 1784, death came to Phillis Wheatley, the first Negro woman in America to become an author.

Paul Cuffe. This successful businessman was interested in improving opportunities for Negroes. He was born of free parents near New Bedford, Massachusetts, in 1759. Like many Massachusetts boys, young Paul Cuffe had a love for the sea. He became a sailor on a trading vessel while he was still in his teens. Then he dared to dream big dreams. He wanted to be a shipowner, and he was willing to work to make his dream come true. He built his first small sailing ship himself. In time, he became the owner of several ships, the largest of which was the 268-ton *Alpha*. This ship, manned by an all-Negro crew, carried supplies back and forth from America to countries in Europe. Paul Cuffe was a rich man for the times in which he lived. His fortune at one time was worth $20,000.

Paul Cuffe was interested in being more than a successful shipowner. He worked to improve the conditions under which free Negroes lived. When he was just nineteen years old, he and his brother sued in court for the right to vote. He pointed out that he paid taxes and as a tax-payer, he should have the right to vote. He lost his case, but his action called attention to the fact that free Negroes were not permitted to vote. Five years later, in 1783, Massachusetts passed a law extending the right to vote to free Negroes.

Paul Cuffe acted to solve another problem in his community. There were no schools for Negro children in New Bedford, and Negroes were not permitted to attend schools established for white children. Paul Cuffe remembered that he had taught himself to read and write when he was in his teens. Years later, there were still no schools that his own children could attend. Knowing from experience the importance of education, Paul Cuffe had a small schoolhouse built on his own farm, hired a teacher, and paid the salary himself. Then he opened the doors of the school to all Negro children in New Bedford.

In the early 1800's, some people became interested in a new idea. They believed that the free Negroes would be happier if they left the United States and started their own colony in Africa. Negroes, for the most part, were opposed to this idea of colonization. They felt that this was their own country and that the problems they faced could be worked out. The idea of a free colony in Africa, however, interested Paul Cuffe. In 1811, he sailed to

Sierra Leone, a small British colony on the western coast of Africa where Great Britain settled former slaves. While he was there, he made arrangements to establish a special colony called the Friendly Society for American Negroes. In 1815, using one of his own ships, Paul Cuffe took the first colonists to the Friendly Society in Sierra Leone. There were thirty-eight settlers, each looking for a better life. Plans had been made to send other interested Negroes to the colony but Paul Cuffe died in 1817 and interest in this colonization scheme died with him. Paul Cuffe, the successful businessman, used his own money and time to try to solve some of the Negroes' problems.

James Derham.   From slave, to Revolutionary War soldier, to doctor—that was the story of James Derham's life. James Derham was born a slave in Philadelphia in 1762. He grew up in the household of a master who was a doctor. The boy was intelligent and as he reached his teens, he was given training in the mixing of medicines by the doctor who owned him. He went with the doctor on his calls and learned much through observation. During the period of the Revolutionary War, James Derham was sold to another doctor. This man was a surgeon who took his slave with him when he served in the Continental Army. This experience gave young Derham the chance to learn even more about medicine. After the war, there was another change of masters for James Derham. Dr. Robert Dove took this talented young slave with him to New Orleans. Impressed with the ability of James Derham, Dr. Dove permitted the slave to earn his freedom on easy terms. Dr. Dove did more than that. He helped his former slave get started in the practice of medicine. James Derham became a successful and respected doctor who treated both Negro and white patients in New Orleans. He was the first Negro doctor in the United States.

Richard Allen.   This great religious leader spent his whole life in helping his people. He was born into slavery. When he was a young man, his master allowed him to hire himself out and work for wages. By hard work, Richard Allen was able to save two thousand dollars, the price that he paid for his freedom. This was probably more than four times what a slave cost then. When free to choose his own work, Richard Allen followed his interest in religious matters. As a slave, he had been deeply moved by the words of Methodist ministers who had preached at his master's farm. He, himself, had tried preaching to the other slaves.

As a free man, Richard Allen was chosen to go with a traveling minister and help him with the services. The two men traveled through Pennsylvania, New Jersey, and Maryland, holding religious meetings in many small villages and farms. After some time, Richard Allen became a preacher in his own right. Traveling alone with no helper, he brought the religious message to many small communities. This was a hard life, and after a number of years Richard Allen stopped traveling and came to live in Philadelphia in 1786.

At this time, there were no separate churches for Negroes. Richard Allen attended the St. George Methodist Episcopal Church in Philadelphia and preached there on one occasion. He was disturbed by the prejudice that Negroes experienced in the church. Negroes were permitted to sit only upstairs. Once during prayer, Richard Allen and a friend knelt down at the front of the balcony to pray. They were rudely ordered to move to the back of the room but waited until the prayer was finished before they moved. When the prayer was over, they did not go to the back of the room but walked out of the church itself.

That incident started Richard Allen's dream of a separate church for Negroes. Its Negro leaders and officers would be in complete control of the church life. Allen started by holding prayer meetings for Negroes, which were well attended. Then in 1787, he worked with other Negro leaders to organize the Free African Society. This organization worked hard to give help where it was needed. Money was given to the needy, widows received insurance, and the education of Negro children was financed. The Free African Society also gave Negroes a chance to meet together and try to work out their own problems. It was the first time that Negroes in America had joined together in an organization to help themselves.

Then in 1793, the Free African Society gave help to all the citizens of Philadelphia, not just to Negroes. From August to the end of October, a deadly plague raged in the city. It was yellow fever, and as many as twenty-four people a day died from the disease. Many left the city, trying to find safety. Doctors and nurses worked to the point of exhaustion and still were not able to care for all of the sick. Richard Allen and other leaders of the Free African Society visited the mayor of Philadelphia. They said that the members of the Society would help in whatever way they could. Negroes volunteered as nurses; they moved the sick to temporary hospitals; they drove the dead to cemeteries and buried them; some were trained to give medical care to the patients. They served until the epidemic was over in November, and their work during the plague was long remembered.

Richard Allen and the bishops of his new church.

Richard Allen started to organize an independent church. In 1794, he and other free Negroes started the Bethel African Methodist Episcopal Church. From the beginning, the church was a success, growing in strength and influence. It established a night school for adults and a day school for children. It became a model for independent Negro churches in other cities.

In 1816, Richard Allen took another step forward by planning for sixteen independent Negro churches to join into a national organization. This organization became the African Methodist Episcopal Church, and Richard Allen was chosen as its first bishop. This was a deserved honor for the man who made the independent church such a strong influence in Negro life.

From Revolutionary War

to Civil War

Slavery had become firmly established in the agricultural states of the South by the early 1800's. Thousands of workers were needed to plant and hoe and harvest the cotton crop. The slaves, who provided that work, had little chance to express their true feelings about their lives. If they were unhappy, they did not dare to say so, for slaves who complained were usually punished. So they sang about their troubles, and the words of the songs plainly showed their sorrow and their hopes for freedom in the future.

> Nobody knows the trouble I've seen
> Nobody knows but Jesus.

> Go down, Moses, way down in Egypt land,
> Tell old Pharaoh to let my people go.

> Didn't my Lord deliver Daniel
> And why not every man?

Sometimes individual slaves protested their situations by slowing down their work; some pretended to be ill. Others tried to run away, but escape was difficult. Most slaves knew little about the countryside beyond the plantations where they worked. They were easily recognized by anyone who might see them, and there was no one to help them. Even if a slave succeeded in reaching another state, he was not safe. The Fugitive (runaway) Slave Law, passed in 1793, said that runaway slaves must be returned to their masters.

Slave Revolts

Between 1800 and 1831, there were three major well-planned revolts against slavery and many minor ones. Each major revolt was led by a Negro who planned to raise an army of slaves to overcome the planters. The leader of each revolt meant to use force to gain freedom for the slaves.

Gabriel Prosser in Virginia

A Virginia slave, Gabriel Prosser, had visions of freeing many slaves who lived close to Richmond. In 1800, he made his plans for a surprise attack on the city of Richmond. There, he and his army of slaves would get weapons with which to continue the revolt. Prosser developed his plans in the greatest of secrecy. He got more than a thousand slaves to join in the project. But just before the attack took place, news of the plan leaked out. Two house slaves who knew of the plot felt a loyalty to the families they served. These two told their masters about the revolt and their masters told the authorities. Prosser and other leaders of the revolt were captured, tried, and put to death.

Denmark Vesey in South Carolina

In 1822, Denmark Vesey, a former slave who had bought his own freedom, planned a revolt in South Carolina. Vesey worked as a carpenter in Charleston, and he wished to gain for other slaves the freedom he had bought for himself. He made careful plans for a revolt, selected trustworthy leaders, and enlisted slaves who were willing to fight for their freedom. But once again, house slaves reported the plot. Vesey and the other leaders of the revolt were arrested, found guilty, and put to death.

Nat Turner in Virginia

The biggest and bloodiest revolt was led by Nat Turner, a Virginia slave preacher. Turner worked as a field hand by day and preached to his fellow slaves in the evenings and on Sundays. He was a deeply religious man who claimed to see visions and hear voices. Convinced that he had been called by God to lead his people out of bondage, Nat Turner gathered together a small group of followers and organized a revolt which he and six companions initiated on August 21, 1831, by killing every member of his master's family—man, woman, and child. Moving on to other plantations, that night and the next day Turner and about sixty followers killed fifty-seven people, most of them children. Panic-stricken, some of the white citizens banded together to suppress the rebellion. Turner fled to the swamps and hid for almost two months before he was captured. He and the leaders of the revolt were brought to trial and hanged.

Results of the Slave Revolts

The Turner revolt brought a wave of terror to the South. Many plantation families in Virginia felt unsafe as long as Turner was still in hiding. Some left their plantations and moved into cities to live until Turner was captured. They were determined that the slaves would not revolt again, while many thousands of slaves were still determined to be free.

Plantation owners throughout the South watched over their slaves very closely, to keep them isolated from men like Turner. Slaves from neighboring plantations could not meet together in large groups. Negro preachers were not allowed to talk to the slaves except when a member of the master's family was present. Many of the religious services were led by white ministers who urged the slaves to be obedient and serve their masters well. Since the planters felt that educated slaves would become more discontented with their lives, laws were passed forbidding the teaching of any slave to read or write. These laws, however, were not always obeyed or enforced. Slaveholders felt that restrictions like

A white family supervising while a Negro preaches to slaves.

these lessened the danger of future revolts; but they were mistaken, for slave revolts continued despite their endeavors.

Free Negroes

During the early 1800's, free Negroes as well as slaves faced restrictions. They did not have the same personal liberty that other citizens took for granted. In the South, for example, free Negroes had to carry official certificates of their freedom at all times. The certificate proved that its owner was not a runaway slave. Most southern states did not allow freemen to travel beyond the county in which they lived. Free Negroes also faced the possibility of being kidnaped and sold into slavery. If they were found guilty of breaking laws, their sentences might involve a return to slavery.

In the northern states free Negroes found the same situation of limited freedom. The free Negro was not allowed to vote in most states. If he owned property, he paid taxes for schools which his children were not allowed to attend. Before Negroes could live in certain northern states, they had to pay a sum of money to buy their way in. Ohio, for example, required free Negroes to pay a $500 bond as a guarantee of their good behavior.

Ways of Earning a Living

In spite of restrictions, many Negroes were able to make a comfortable living. In the South, they followed as many as fifty different types of occupations. Some made clothing, piloted ships, or processed foods. There were Negro ministers, druggists, grocers, barbers, shoemakers, carpenters, and brickmasons. In South Carolina, Jehu Jones was an unusual example of a successful businessman. This Negro hotel owner is said to have had property that was worth $40,000.

Northern free Negroes usually lived in large cities where there were greater opportunities for earning a comfortable living. In trying to find work, however, the Negro worker faced discrimination. He had to compete with white workers to get the better jobs and often lost, merely because of his color.

During the early 1800's, free Negroes in the North worked in a hundred different skilled jobs. Besides the skilled workers, there were professional workers: ministers, teachers, dentists, and lawyers. Others worked as paper hangers, engravers, restaurant owners, and tailors. A few Negroes became quite rich. James Forten, a factory owner, is said to have amassed as much as $100,000. He hired both Negro and white workers to make sails in his factory in Philadelphia.

The American Colonization Society

Although the free Negro could make a living in the United States, he did not enjoy the same privileges as other citizens. From time to time, the idea of returning Negroes to Africa was reconsidered. In 1817, a group of prominent men including John C.

Calhoun and Henry Clay formed the American Colonization Society to carry out this plan. Land would be bought in Africa, and a colony established for free American Negroes. The Society raised money by public and private contribution, persuading the United States Congress to give hundreds of thousands of dollars for the plan, and the colony of Liberia on the west coast of Africa came into being.

The first boatload of settlers arrived in Liberia in 1822. All of them were free Negroes, but later settlers were apt to be recently freed slaves. By 1827, a number of slaves were even being given their freedom on the condition that they would move to Liberia, and from that time on, more newly freed slaves settled in the African colony than did free-born Negroes. In 1847, the colony of Liberia became an independent country. Its name came from the word liberty, and its capital city, Monrovia, was named after President James Monroe.

In spite of the efforts of the American Colonization Society, the majority of American Negroes remained in the United States. By 1852, only about eight thousand of the three and a half million Negroes in the country had left to start a new life in Liberia. Most Negroes were deeply concerned about the problems of slavery and discrimination. Free Negroes and anti-slavery whites had attacked the Society's idea of relocation from its very beginning. Instead of leaving the country, the Negroes, with help from white sympathizers, would try to improve disagreeable conditions at home.

The Convention Movement

Free Negroes, particularly those in the North, were disturbed by the problems Negroes faced. Leaders like Richard Allen and James Forten organized annual conventions for Negroes. The aims of the conventions were to bring an end to slavery and to fight against discrimination in the North. The first Negro convention was held in Philadelphia in 1831, the same year as the Turner revolt. Speeches were made, and articles written about slavery. The conventions met each year in different northern cities. In

1853, the Negro convention published the following statement: "We ask that in our native land we shall not be treated as strangers, and worse than strangers." [1] At other times, the conventions sent petitions to Congress requesting freedom for the slaves. Their protests against slavery and discrimination continued through the Civil War years and won the support and friendship of many citizens.

War of 1812

In 1812 when the United States was at war with Great Britain, the call for soldiers went out. Free Negroes were urged to enlist in both the Army and Navy. As had been the case during the Revolutionary War, freedom was promised to slaves who served in the armed forces.

One of the naval battles of this war took place on Lake Erie under the leadership of Captain Oliver Perry. When the battle was over, Perry made his famous victory statement, "We have met the enemy, and they are ours." Perry also praised the courage of the Negro seamen, especially the bravery of John Johnson, who was killed in action. His commander said of him, "When America has such tars, she has little to fear from the tyrants of the ocean." [2]

Negroes also saw action in the famous Battle of New Orleans under General Andrew Jackson. Two battalions of Negro soldiers took part in the furious fighting that resulted in an overwhelming American victory. Andrew Jackson praised the courage of all of his soldiers. He sent this message to the Negro troops, "I invited you to share in the perils and to divide the glory of your white countrymen. I expected much from you. . . . But you surpassed my hopes. . . . The President of the United States shall be informed of your conduct on the present occasion." [3]

[1] Benjamin Quarles, *The Negro in the Making of America* (New York: Collier Books, 1967), p. 103.

[2] Carter Woodson and Charles Wesley, *The Story of the Negro Retold* (Washington, D.C.: The Associated Publishers, Inc., 1959), p. 90.

[3] *Ibid.,* p. 91.

Westward Expansion

During the 1800's, more and more settlers moved westward across the Appalachian Mountains. They lived as pioneers in the western land gained from Great Britain after the Revolutionary War. When there were enough settlers in a region to form a state, the new state would be admitted to the Union. Many of the people who moved into the land south of the Ohio River made their living by farming. They used slaves as workers on farms and plantations. The new states in this territory became slave states. The land north of the Ohio River was located in the Northwest Territory where slavery was forbidden under the terms of the Northwest Ordinance. New states north of the Ohio River became free states. Like New England, these states developed many industries, and farming became less important to their life.

It is easy to see that two strong sections were developing in our country, and that each section had a different idea about slavery. The southern states, which were mainly agricultural, felt that slavery was necessary to their plantation system. The industrial states of the North were opposed to slavery.

This was seen more clearly when the United States gained new western land. In 1803, the United States bought the Louisiana Territory from France. By the end of the Mexican War in 1848, the United States owned land that stretched as far west as the Pacific Ocean. When these new territories were opened for settlement, the question of slavery again presented problems. Southern planters, who wished to buy rich land for raising cotton in the new territories, needed slaves to carry out the work. On the other hand, some settlers from the northern states felt that slavery should not be permitted in the new lands. For a time, each section was able to solve these differences through compromise or through working together toward an agreement.

Action of Congress

Between 1820 and 1854, Congress passed three important laws concerning slavery and the western territories. They were the Missouri Compromise, the Compromise of 1850, and the Kansas–Nebraska Act of 1854. Each of the laws tried to settle the question of whether slave states or free states should be formed in the western regions.

The Missouri Compromise dealt with slavery in the Louisiana Territory. Congress decided that the territory should be divided into two sections, one slave and one free. Any new state formed north of the dividing line would be free, and any state formed south of the line would be slave. By this act, Congress reduced the spread of slavery in the Louisiana Territory.

In 1848 at the end of the Mexican War, the United States gained another huge tract of land. Once more the question was

How the United States was divided by three slavery rulings.

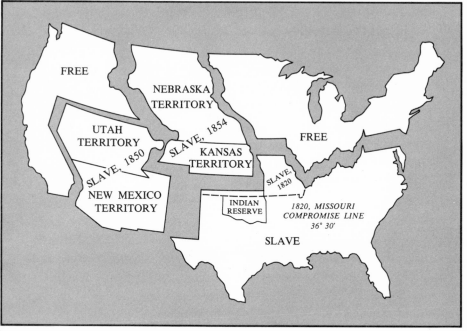

raised: would future states in the new territory be slave or free? Two years later, Congress passed the Compromise of 1850 to answer that question. The Compromise of 1850 granted California the right to become a free state. This law also stated that the settlers who lived in the new region should themselves decide about slavery. When there were enough people to form a state, these persons should vote on whether their new state should be slave or free. This law was passed to try to please both sections of the country. It gave to the people the responsibility of settling the slavery question.

The third law, the Kansas–Nebraska Act, dealt once more with slavery in the Louisiana Territory. It was concerned especially with the northern sections of this region, Kansas and Nebraska. Some of the settlers who had moved into this land were dissatisfied with the Missouri Compromise. They objected to the dividing line which separated slave territory from free lands. Some of the people who had settled north of the dividing line wanted a chance to decide for themselves about slavery. In 1854, Congress passed the Kansas–Nebraska Act. This law allowed the settlers who lived in the territory to make their own decision about slavery. When this law was passed, the dividing line of the Missouri Compromise no longer had any effect.

Dred Scott Case—1857

Eventually, the Supreme Court of the United States also became involved with the problem of slavery. In 1857, the Supreme Court gave a decision that slaves could not become citizens of the United States. This decision was the result of the famous *Dred Scott* case.

Dred Scott, a slave, had been taken by his master from Missouri to free territory in the North. After living there for some time, the family returned to Missouri. Upon his return, Dred Scott stated that he should be a free man. His reason was that he had lived for some time in a free territory where slavery was not permitted. Friends helped him take his case to court, and it finally reached the Supreme Court of the United States.

Dred Scott

The Supreme Court ruled that Dred Scott was not free, but a slave. As a slave, he had none of the rights of a citizen. As a slave, he was only property. In addition, the Court ruled that Congress had no power to exclude slavery from the Territories.

Negroes in the Westward Expansion

While these decisions were being reached by the Congress and Supreme Court, Negroes were moving into the western territories. Many went as slaves, but some went as free men. Frontier living was difficult, and a man's courage and strength were often more important than his background. For this reason, many of the Negro pioneers enjoyed more freedom in the western lands. They worked as miners, fur traders, explorers, and carpenters. The lives of three men will show the kinds of contributions Negroes made to the growing West.

George Bush.   This adventurous man wanted to know what lay beyond the mountains in the western lands. He was an explorer who delighted in pushing forward into unknown regions. By 1820, he had reached the Pacific coast and had explored the land north of the Columbia River. He liked what he saw and decided that he would like to live there in the future.

In 1842, he started west again with his family, traveling over the Oregon Trail. He bought land in the Oregon Territory. Some authorities say that he built the first sawmill and grist mill on Puget Sound. When George Bush saw other pioneers moving into the Oregon wilderness, he remembered his own struggles in getting started on the frontier. He offered practical help to the new settlers, giving them food and other needed supplies. Through his own ability, he made a satisfactory life for himself and his family. Like a true pioneer, he helped his neighbors.

James Beckwourth.   One of a colorful group of men known as the mountain men, James Beckwourth was a trapper, explorer, guide, scout, Indian fighter, and a teller of tall tales. He knew the mountains and valleys of the West, from Missouri to the Pacific coast. He knew Indian customs, too, and could speak the languages of three different Indian tribes. He lived for years with the Crow Indians and was made a chieftain of their tribe.

Like all mountain men, Jim Beckwourth delighted in telling tales of his adventures and narrow escapes. To make the stories more exciting, he exaggerated some of the details. Twenty Indians on the warpath might grow into two hundred in Jim Beckwourth's stories. One of the adventures found in his autobiography tells of a race for life. Beckwourth was working with a group of trappers.

Some of their horses had wandered from the camp, and Jim Beck-wourth and a companion went out to hunt for them. The men tracked the horses all that day, and at night they camped in a thicket. As they started out at dawn the next morning, they were followed by a band of "between two and three hundred Indians." Beckwourth's companion played safe and hid in the thicket. However, Jim Beckwourth decided to try to outrun the Indians and reach the main camp of the trappers. He ran "as swift as an antelope," keeping well ahead of the Indians who pounded after him. On and on they tore. Finally he reached the place where the trappers had camped two days before. To his dismay, the camp was deserted; the trapping party had moved on. Jim Beckwourth's only hope was to continue with the race. Now the Indians were close enough so that their bullets whizzed by his head. On and on he ran. At last he saw the welcome sight of campfire smoke. He had caught up with the trappers, who had seen the danger and had come on horseback. They turned back the Indians, and Jim Beckwourth's scalp was saved. He ended his story with this statement: "According to the closest calculation, I ran that day ninety-five miles." [4] This was a true tall tale, told in the style of the mountain men!

While searching for gold in California, James Beckwourth discovered a pass, or low place, in the Sierra Nevada Mountains. He realized that the settlers moving west would be able to cross the high mountains more easily if they knew about this pass. He helped raise money to clear a wagon trail through the pass, and he himself guided a wagon train along the route he had discovered. In time, many settlers going to California used Beckwourth Pass, which even today honors the name of its discoverer.

Barney Ford. Born a slave in Virginia in 1822, Barney Ford grew up to serve as a waiter on Mississippi River boats. Eventually he ran away to Chicago where he helped other runaway

---

[4] James Beckwourth, *Life and Adventures of James P. Beckwourth* (New York: Alfred A. Knopf, Inc., 1931), pp. 81–82.

slaves find homes. In the 1850's Ford went to Central America, to Nicaragua, where he built and ran two hotels. With money saved, he returned to Chicago and there heard exciting stories of gold discoveries in the American West.

In 1860 he arrived in Denver to try his luck in the gold fields nearby. He did not get rich from gold but eventually went into the banking and hotel businesses in Denver. His most famous hotel, the Inter-Ocean in Denver, was known as the finest and most elegant stopping place between St. Louis and San Francisco. He sold it in 1874 for $75,000.

Barney Ford was more than a successful businessman. He worked to improve opportunities for Negroes in Colorado. With other leading citizens of Denver, he worked to have Colorado admitted into the Union as a state.

The Abolitionist Movement

During this period, from 1800 to 1860, the condition of slavery was being treated differently in various parts of the country. It was firmly established in the South. In the North, free Negroes were working together to improve conditions for all their people. At the same time, slavery in the western territories caused disagreements between the people who lived in the North and those who lived in the South. While these things were happening, an important movement was organized, the abolitionist movement. The words *abolitionist* and *abolition* have the same root as *abolish,* which means to "do away with." Abolitionists were persons who wanted to do away with slavery and grant freedom to the slaves.

The abolitionist movement was made up of many different kinds of people. Some were white and some Negro. Some were well educated; some were not. Some lived in the North, others in the South. Some individuals made speeches, and others wrote articles. Even though their backgrounds were different, they all worked for the same cause.

Southern White Abolitionists

In the South, the system of slavery was closely tied together with the way the people made their living. In order to raise large amounts of cotton, as well as tobacco and sugar, southern planters needed two things: many acres of land and many workers. They bought the land they needed and they bought slaves to do the work. If the abolitionists succeeded and the slaves were freed, the southern planters would lose most of their wealth. They would lose, first of all, the sum of money that they had originally paid for the slaves. They would lose the labor of the slaves. Without this cheap labor, the work of the huge plantations could not be maintained and because of this, many southerners were violently opposed to abolition. But the majority of southern citizens did not own slaves. Some of them did not believe in slavery and spoke out against the whole system.

Elihu Embree. A resident of Tennessee, Elihu Embree was a businessman and a slave owner. In 1812, he became a Quaker. One of the Quaker beliefs, that all people are equal, had such a strong influence on Elihu Embree that he granted freedom to his own slaves. Then he became an active abolitionist, trying to interest others in following his example. In 1820 he published a weekly newspaper, the *Emancipator,* in which he wrote articles that encouraged the abolition of slavery. His paper was one of the first abolitionist newspapers in the entire country. The theme of the articles of this newspaper never changed; it was "Liberty for all persons."

John Fee. As a child, John Fee lived on a plantation in Kentucky. Since his father owned slaves, young John accepted their presence without question. When John Fee decided to become a minister, he was sent to study in Cincinnati. At Lane Seminary there, Fee met people who were part of the abolitionist movement. For the first time in his life, he began to think seriously about the question of slavery. He finally reached the conclusion that holding slaves was against all Christian teachings. He decided then not only to become a minister, but also to preach against slavery. Moreover, he was determined to do this in his own slave state of Kentucky in spite of all the difficulties he knew he would face.

John Fee met his first problem when he told his family of this decision. His father was furious and threatened to disown the boy if he continued with the plan. John Fee showed that he was serious by walking out of his father's house, never to return. After that, his life seemed full of difficulties. He tried to establish churches where he could preach, but no one seemed to want to hear his message. He moved to the central part of Kentucky where he was given land for a church by Cassius Clay, a wealthy Kentuckian who was also opposed to slavery. On this land, John Fee worked to establish a special community in which a church and a school would serve all races. The community was named Berea. Under great difficulty, he started a school called the Berea Academy. Negro and white pupils studied together at the academy in spite of the disapproval of the neighboring slaveholders. In 1858, the first commencement exercises of this unusual school were held. In this year also, Berea was reorganized as a college which offered higher education to all. The motto of the college was the Bible verse, "God has made of one blood all nations of men."

During the Civil War, Berea College was closed temporarily. At the end of the war, John Fee returned to Berea. Here he worked with other interested persons to open the college doors once more. Steady progress was made from that time. Berea College accepted as students all persons of good moral character. Progress in integrated schooling was halted, however, in 1904, when Kentucky passed a state law which segregated the races in schools. A second and separate college, Lincoln Institute, was built for the Negro students by the friends of Berea.

John Fee, the son of a southern slaveholder, devoted his entire life to the idea of brotherhood. He was not content merely to preach about brotherhood. Through his actions, he put his ideas into practice and gave many people the opportunity for self-improvement.

Northern White Abolitionists

The South's one-crop system of agriculture, which called for unskilled labor, never developed in the North, and so slavery had gradually been abolished in these states. Northerners knew that if abolition came, they would not lose a fortune. Their whole system of earning a living would not be thrown into confusion. They were freer to act against slavery than were the southerners whose money was tied up in the ownership of slaves.

White abolitionists in the North worked to bring an end to slavery. They all felt that slavery was wrong, but they held different ideas about how to abolish it. Some abolitionists thought that the slave owners should be paid for the slaves that were freed. Other abolitionists thought no payment should be made. The work of the abolitionists was carried out through speeches, through writing, and through action. Poets like Henry Wadsworth Longfellow and John Greenleaf Whittier wrote poems against slavery. Prudence Crandall, a Connecticut school teacher, went to jail because she admitted a Negro girl into her school. The efforts of all the abolitionists gave publicity to the idea of freedom for all.

William Lloyd Garrison. As a newspaperman, William Lloyd Garrison wrote and spoke in a stirring manner. One of the most influential of the workers for abolition, he started a newspaper, the *Liberator,* in 1831. During the first years that the *Liberator* was printed, the majority of its readers were Negroes. The paper spoke out boldly against slavery and urged the immediate freeing of all slaves. Some people in both the North and the South were alarmed by the outspoken ideas printed in the paper. Garrison was accused of stirring up trouble, and at one time, his printing press was broken up by a group of angry citizens. He simply continued printing the paper and thought of even more ways to work for the abolitionist cause.

William Lloyd Garrison was also an outstanding speaker, and he made many talks against slavery. In 1833, he worked with others to establish the American Antislavery Society in the city of Philadelphia. In pamphlets and books, he wrote about some of the accomplishments of outstanding Negroes. He often pointed out that under slavery Negroes could accomplish little. Once given freedom and the opportunity, they could make important contributions to their communities.

James Birney.   Although born in Kentucky, James Birney lived in Cincinnati when he printed *The Philanthropist,* another antislavery newspaper. Like William Garrison's *Liberator, The Philanthropist* contained articles, sermons, poems, and quotations from speeches—all against slavery. Some people who did not believe in abolition regarded James Birney as a troublemaker. In 1836, a group of these angry people stormed into his newly established newspaper office and destroyed the printing press. James Birney got new presses and printed a few more issues of *The Philanthropist* before he closed down his operation and left Cincinnati in 1837. He became secretary of the American Antislavery Society in New York City.

Negro Abolitionists

Negroes also took an active part in the abolitionist movement. Many of the outstanding Negroes of this period were not content to improve only their own lives. They joined the efforts of other abolitionists to try to gain freedom for all Negroes. They worked in the same way by making speeches, preaching sermons, printing newspapers, and writing books. They were active, also, in forming antislavery societies. By 1830, fifty of these societies, organized by Negroes, were in active existence. There were Negro abolitionists who served on the executive committees of the American Antislavery Society.

Some of the Negro abolitionists had been free all of their lives, while others had lived under slavery. Some had had the chance to get a fine education, while others had learned to read and write through their own efforts. But the work of all of them in the antislavery movement made many people aware of the talents and abilities of Negroes.

David Walker was one of the first writers to become prominent as an abolitionist. In 1829, he printed a pamphlet called *Appeal* in which the unjust conditions of slavery were described in detail. The *Appeal* also denounced American Christians for allowing slavery to exist and called upon all slaves to rise up and revolt against their masters. This pamphlet had a wide circulation.

Two other writers became well known for printing the first Negro newspaper in America. They were Samuel Cornish, a minister, and John Russwurm, who had the unusual advantage of a college education. John Russwurm, who completed his studies at Bowdoin College in 1826, was the first Negro college graduate in the United States. He and Samuel Cornish started the newspaper *Freedom's Journal* in 1827.

Frederick Douglass. The greatest of all the Negro abolitionists, Frederick Douglass was an outstanding speaker, newspaper editor, and author. During his lifetime, he had an interview with President Lincoln and he was appointed to positions of political service.

Frederick Douglass was born in Maryland in 1817, a slave. When only ten years old, he was sent to Baltimore to serve in the house of one of his master's relatives. His new mistress started to teach him to read, but the lessons were stopped when the master of the house forbade them. The idea of reading had opened a whole new world for the boy who continued to read when alone. There were times when he played with white boys of the neighborhood, and he often asked these playmates to help him with difficult words. He learned to write by copying letters and words that he saw in books. At night in his own room, he spent hours poring over the Bible and a hymn book, his only textbooks. During this time in his life, Frederick began to yearn for freedom. He rebelled against the idea of being a slave, of never being free. He later wrote in his autobiography, "It was not my enslavement at the then present time which most affected me—the *being a slave for life* was the saddest thought." [5]

[5] Frederick Douglass, *The Life and Times of Frederick Douglass,* revised (New York: Collier Books, 1962), p. 92.

Frederick Douglass

In time, Frederick Douglass served in other homes, some of which were more harsh than the one in Baltimore. He was twenty-one before he had the chance to escape. With the help of friends, he obtained a sailor's uniform and a protection paper that he would show to anyone who might question him. In this disguise, he rode a train to New York and freedom. He later moved to Boston, and in this city he started his work as an abolitionist. Frederick Douglass had read many copies of William Garrison's *Liberator*. He finally met William Garrison, who encouraged him to speak to an audience about his experiences under slavery. It was a touching speech, and the audience was spellbound. From that time on, Frederick Douglass was in demand as a speaker against slavery. He was successful in making people feel the injustices of slavery.

In 1845, Frederick Douglass went to England where he lived for two years, making speeches and winning friends for the abolitionist cause. While he was in England, he was able to raise some money for a project of his own. When he returned to the United States in 1848, he bought his freedom.

After establishing a home in Rochester, New York, Frederick Douglass tried a new type of work. He started a newspaper which he called *The North Star*. The name had a significant meaning. Frederick Douglass knew that slaves who were trying to run away from their plantations traveled only at night under the protection of darkness. They had no maps, but they looked for the North Star to guide them north to freedom. He hoped his paper would be a guide toward freedom for Negroes. The newspaper was a success, but there were other papers with the same name. So Douglass renamed his paper *The Frederick Douglass Paper*. He also wrote an autobiography, *The Narrative of Frederick Douglass*. In the book he described his experiences as a slave, his feelings about slavery, and his hopes and ambitions for the Negro as a free citizen. Through his writings and speeches and because of his wisdom and experience, Frederick Douglass became the most influential Negro of the late 1800's. He was the leader of his own race and was respected by all people.

During the troubled times of the Civil War, Frederick Douglass gave patriotic service to his country. He helped recruit soldiers for the Union Army. He met with President Lincoln to discuss the problems faced by Negro soldiers. He was present at the reception after President Lincoln's second inauguration.

After the Civil War, Frederick Douglass continued to serve his country. He was appointed to the following important positions: Commissioner to Haiti, Recorder of Deeds for the District of Columbia, United States Marshal for the District of Columbia, and Minister to Haiti. Returning to Washington, D.C., he bought a beautiful home, Cedar Hill, which was located in Anacostia, D.C. Frederick Douglass spent the last thirteen years of his life in this twenty-room colonial style house. Recently dedicated as a national shrine, his home still contains some of the original furniture, including a desk that was given to Frederick Douglass by Harriet Beecher Stowe.

Frederick Douglass constantly expressed the hope of the Negro people to become full citizens. He wrote this idea in clear words: "What I ask for the Negro is not benevolence, not pity, not sympathy, but simple justice. . . . If the Negro cannot stand on his own legs, let him fall. All I ask, give him a chance to stand on his own legs. Let him alone! If you see him on his way to school, let him alone! If you see him going to the ballot box, let him alone! If you see him going into a workshop, let him alone! If you will only untie his hands and give him a chance, I think he will live." [6]

Sojourner Truth.   Another dramatic speaker against slavery was Sojourner Truth, a tall, gaunt woman who could neither read nor write. Sojourner Truth had been born a slave, named Isabella, but she had managed to run away from her owners in upstate New York. Later, she had become free under New York's Emancipation Act of July 4th, 1827. She was a deeply religious woman who had a strange experience during which she seemed to be called into a new life. She said, "I felt so tall within—I felt as if the power of the nation was with me." [7]

Isabella took on the new name of Sojourner Truth. She believed her Lord had called her to sojourn, or travel, across the land speaking the truth as she saw it. Her speeches had a great impact on both Negro and white audiences, for the message that she presented was both dramatic and sincere. Her voice was deep, and she spoke in the dialect of the simple ex-slave. Across her chest she wore a banner with the words "Proclaim liberty throughout the land unto all the inhabitants thereof." These are the same stirring words that are engraved on the Liberty Bell.

Sojourner Truth showed her patriotism during the Civil War by working with the Union Army as a lookout and a spy. She was received by President Lincoln at the White House. At that time,

[6] Merl Eppse, *The Negro, Too, in American History* (Nashville: The National Publishing Company, Inc., 1943), p. 179.
[7] Russell Adams, *Great Negroes Past and Present* (Chicago: Afro-Am Publishing Company, Inc., 1964), p. 25.

Sojourner Truth with President Abraham Lincoln.

she presented him with a Bible given to him by the Negroes of
Baltimore.

The Underground Railroad

Perhaps no way of helping runaway slaves was more dramatic
than the assistance given by the Underground Railroad. Because
of the adventure and dangers involved, many legends have grown
up about its operation. It has been difficult to separate legend
from fact.

The Underground Railroad was not a railroad at all. Rather,
it was a system of helping escaping slaves reach safety. Made up
of individuals, it consisted of a series of houses or safe hiding
places called stations. According to legend, when the runaway
reached the first station, his chances for freedom were certain. He
would automatically be fed and sheltered by "conductors" of the
Underground Railroad. More important, he would be taken to
the next station, and then to the next, usually at night. Finally
with the help of many conductors, the slave would reach Canada
and safety. Early histories follow the legend that slaves made little
effort to help themselves once they were under the protection of
the Underground Railroad.

Recent research, however, has shown that early accounts of the
Underground Railroad were not always accurate. Many of the
slaves who escaped actually received little or no assistance. Often
they traveled for weeks at a time with no help of any kind. Traveling at night, avoiding contact with any person, some escaping
slaves knew nothing about the work of the Underground Railroad. Their flight to freedom was the result of their own efforts
and courage.

Other runaways were told about sympathetic individuals who
would help. Accidentally learning about the Underground Railroad in this manner, they were given assistance and safe guidance
to stations farther north. Often after a slave was fed and sheltered,
however, he was merely told about the next safe hiding place. He
had the task of finding the station through his own efforts. He also
ran the risk of being captured while he searched for it.

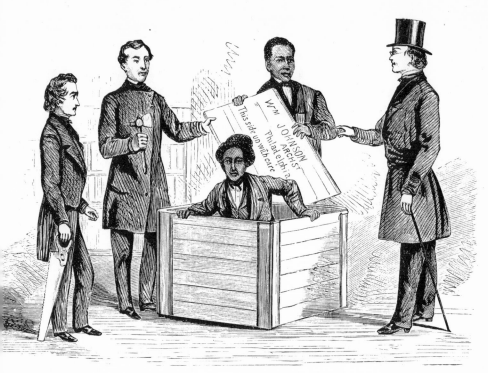

A slave is unpacked from his escape box.

In some communities, though, the work of the Underground Railroad was really active and well organized. Both Negro and white individuals were conductors. As abolitionists, they faced inconvenience and even danger to protect escaping slaves. They were dedicated people who kept on with their work despite danger.

Before 1850, slaves usually felt safe when they reached the northern states. Some made their way to large cities in the North and settled there. Their feeling of safety vanished in 1850, when Congress passed a strict fugitive slave law. According to its terms, any former slave, no matter where he lived in the United States, could be seized and returned to slavery. After 1850, most runaways traveled all the way to Canada to find the freedom they were so desperately seeking.

Harriet Tubman.   Known as the Moses of her race, Harriet Tubman risked her life when she personally led many slaves to freedom. She once stated that as a conductor on the Underground Railroad, she never let the train jump the track and she never lost a single passenger.

Harriet was born in Maryland in 1826, a slave. Even as a little girl, she rebelled against slavery. She once told her parents, "Something inside me won't let me smile at Old Mistress. When she talks to me, I feel all hard inside like I swallowed a stone." When she was a young woman, she found out about the Underground Railroad from a Quaker woman who lived in the village. With help, Harriet managed to escape and went to New York to live. Her first moments of freedom were exciting ones for Harriet. She described her feelings in this way, "I looked at my hands to see if I was the same person now I was free. There was such a glory over everything. The sun came like gold through the trees, and I felt like I was in heaven." [8]

Harriet Tubman was determined to help others have that golden feeling. She herself would return to the plantations, like Moses going into Egypt, and lead them out. She did just this. On her first trip back, her sister, her sister's family, and three others followed her to freedom. There were many other trips and many other people. Harriet made nineteen trips altogether, each one more dangerous than the last. She would announce her presence in the evening by singing, "Go down, Moses," softly outside the slave quarters. Then the exciting news would be whispered from one cabin to the next, "Moses is here!" After dark, there came another song. "Steal away," Harriet sang. That was the signal for all who wanted to follow her to come to the meeting place. In spite of searching parties, in spite of a $40,000 reward for her capture dead or alive, Harriet Tubman led over three hundred people away from slavery.

During the Civil War, Harriet Tubman gave valuable help to the Union Army. She scouted for the army and found information about the strength of Confederate forces. As the war continued,

[8] Dorothy Sterling, *Freedom Train: The Story of Harriet Tubman* (Garden City, New York: Doubleday and Company, Inc., 1954), p. 76.

a need grew for hospital workers to care for the sick and wounded and Harriet Tubman served as a nurse.

William Still.   Unlike Harriet Tubman, who traveled into Maryland to guide her people, William Still remained in Philadelphia, where his house was a station of the Underground Railroad.

William Still was born in Maryland as a slave. While he was a child, his parents fled to the North and eventually lived on a farm in New Jersey. In his twenties, young Still moved to Philadelphia where he started on a program of self-improvement. He taught himself to read and write. He joined the Pennsylvania Abolition Society and in 1847 was made its secretary. It was at this time that he became active in the work of the Underground Railroad. Since he knew the Negro community of Philadelphia so well, he was able to find practical help for large numbers of runaways. His own house was a station, and food, extra clothing, and transportation were often given to those in need. He helped more than six hundred slaves. He kept careful records of their names and destinations so that relatives and friends might have a chance to find them in the future.

William Still worked with others to establish a Negro orphanage where children without parents could be cared for. He was one of the organizers of the first branch of the Y.M.C.A. for Negroes in Philadelphia.

Two Final Abolitionists

Harriet Beecher Stowe.   In 1852, Harriet Beecher Stowe's famous book, *Uncle Tom's Cabin,* was published. The book was an immediate sensation. On the first day it appeared, over three thousand copies were sold.

Uncle Tom's Cabin gave dramatic descriptions of the sufferings and cruel treatment experienced by slaves. The book gave the impression that this was the typical kind of life that all slaves lived, and many readers believed that it was a true picture of slavery. People in the South pointed out that the book did not describe true conditions. Claiming that the episodes were greatly exaggerated, they refused to see that there was some truth, too, in the book. In spite of the differences of opinion, the book was read by hundreds of thousands of people. It was translated into the different languages of Europe and sold there. It was rewritten as a play, and huge audiences wept over the unhappy life of Uncle Tom. Harriet Beecher Stowe's book influenced great numbers of people against slavery. Even President Lincoln recognized the influence of the book. When he met Mrs. Stowe during the Civil War years, some writers say that he remarked, "So this is the little woman who wrote the book that made this great war."

Mrs. Stowe's idea for the character of Uncle Tom was based on a meeting she had with Josiah Henson, an ex-slave. Henson had escaped to Canada where he became active in antislavery work. Working as a minister who made speeches against slavery, he also helped other escaping slaves and wrote a short autobiography. It is possible that Mrs. Stowe had read his book before she met Josiah Henson. After hearing the story of his life, Harriet Beecher Stowe made him the model for Uncle Tom.

John Brown.   In 1859, news of an uprising in Virginia swept through the country. An impatient and devoted abolitionist named John Brown had tried to free the slaves by force.

John Brown had been opposed to slavery all his life. He had fought against it in Kansas and had been active in the Underground Railroad in Ohio. Then he started plans to invade the South and free the slaves by direct action. He tried to interest Frederick Douglass in joining him. Frederick Douglass refused, however, pointing out that the plan was doomed to failure.

John Brown continued working on his plan. On October 16, 1859, he and a few white and Negro followers attacked and captured the United States Armory at Harpers Ferry, Virginia. He had planned to give guns and ammunition from the armory to large numbers of slaves, thinking that they would fight for their own freedom. The slaves never had the chance to join John Brown and his men, as their victory was short. United States troops, led by Colonel Robert E. Lee, were sent to Harpers Ferry where they quickly overpowered the raiders. John Brown and some of his followers were tried for treason because they had attacked government property. They were found guilty and were hanged.

Of the Negroes who followed John Brown, two were killed in fighting the United States troops. Two others were found guilty of treason and were hanged; and one, Osborn Anderson, managed to escape. Later, Osborn Anderson wrote an account of the raid entitled *A Voice from Harpers Ferry.*

After the actions of these last two abolitionists, tension over slavery was running very high throughout the country. It would not be long before differences of opinion broke into open conflict.

A Negro regiment from Massachusetts storms Fort Wagner during the Civil War.

The Civil War

Besides slavery, there were other disagreements between the industrial North and the agricultural South. Some problems that our country faced might have been solved more easily if the nation had been strongly united. The different interests of the two sections made it difficult to reach decisions that pleased both the North and the South.

Conflicts Other Than Slavery

There were two main disagreements between the North and South other than that involving slavery. These were the questions of the tariff and of the strength of the national government.

A tariff is a special tax placed on foreign-made products. Its purpose is to protect home factories from foreign competition. After the War of 1812, when Congress placed a tariff on products made in Great Britain, the nation was again sharply divided. The North, with its many factories, approved of the tariff since it would help keep British-made goods out of America. On the other hand, the farming region of the South was bitterly opposed to it. At one point, the state of South Carolina threatened to *secede from,* or leave, the United States if the tariff was enforced. This action was not carried out, but a dangerous pattern had been set.

The threat of seceding from the Union would be used again with tragic results.

Another point of disagreement between the North and the South concerned the power of the national government. Some people believed that a strong national government was necessary to build a strong country. In their opinion, the Constitution bound all the separate states together into one strong nation. National laws, passed by Congress, would deal with problems faced by the entire country and would be enforced in all of the states. Most northerners believed in strong national government.

Most southerners did not support strong government; they felt each state should have greater power within the limits of the state than did the national government. According to this point of view, the Constitution was merely an agreement among the various states. If any state felt that it had received unjust treatment, then that state could break away from the Union.

The Situation Immediately Before the Civil War

Beside these two other conflicts, the disagreement over slavery continued to divide the country. By 1860 the nation was very near to war.

Extent of Slavery in the South

Not all southerners were slave owners. There were many small farms where the owners and families did the necessary work. In 1860, there were about four million Negro slaves living in the South and about eight million whites. Of the whites only about four hundred thousand, or one in twenty, owned slaves. There were approximately 174,000 persons owning fewer than five slaves. About 165,000 individuals owned from five to fifty slaves. There were a few planters who managed huge plantations with hundreds of slaves. Fifty-six planters owned between three and five hundred slaves, and there were only nine who owned more than five hundred slaves. Clearly, this was a region where great wealth was held by a few individuals.

Election of Lincoln

Abraham Lincoln was the Republican candidate for President in 1860. Recognizing the Constitution as the highest law of the land, he pledged to preserve it and see that it was obeyed in every state of the United States. Although he was concerned about slavery, Lincoln felt his first duty was to keep the country united. He expressed this belief in a speech given in 1858: "A house divided against itself cannot stand. I believe this government cannot endure permanently half-slave and half-free. I do not expect the Union to be dissolved. I do not expect the house to fall, but I do expect it will cease to be divided."

In the South, leaders were disturbed by Lincoln's views on slavery. He had stated clearly at other times that slavery could not be abolished from the southern states where it existed. He had also said, however, that Congress could pass laws to prohibit slavery in the western territories. The southern states threatened to secede from the Union if Lincoln was elected President.

When Lincoln won the election in 1860, South Carolina withdrew from the rest of the nation. Early in 1861, six other states followed. They were Mississippi, Florida, Alabama, Georgia, Louisiana, and Texas. Representatives from these states met and formed a new union, the Confederate States of America. Jefferson Davis was elected president of the newly formed union.

Announcing that it was illegal for the states to secede, President Lincoln pledged that the United States would defend its possessions in the Confederate states. Fort Sumter, at Charleston, South Carolina, was one of the possessions. Fort Sumter was bombarded by the Confederates on April 12, 1861. Fighting continued until the troops at Fort Sumter were forced to surrender on April 14. The first battle of the Civil War had been fought.

President Lincoln sent out a call for troops to preserve the Union and to uphold its laws. The differences between the North and the South had at last led to an actual break between the sections. After Fort Sumter, four additional states left the Union and joined the Confederacy. They were Virginia, Arkansas, North Carolina, and Tennessee. There were some people in these states, however, who remained loyal to the Union.

There were four other slave states that did not secede from the Union. Since they were located close to the North, they were called the border states. The four border states that remained loyal to the Union were Delaware, Maryland, Kentucky, and Missouri. So sides were drawn, and the Civil War, which was to last for four terrible years, began.

Negroes in the Civil War

President Lincoln made the purpose of the Civil War very clear. It was a war to save the Union, to reunite the country. Abolitionists who hoped the war would be fought to end slavery were disappointed with this purpose. Although Lincoln had personal convictions against slavery, he emphasized once more his greatest concern when he wrote to a newspaper editor a full year after the start of the war:

> If I could save the Union without freeing *any* slave, I would do it; and if I could save it by freeing *all* the slaves, I would do it; and if I could save it by freeing some and leaving others alone, I would also do that. What I do about slavery, and the colored race, I do because I believe it helps to save this Union. . . .

When the call for troops was sent out, free Negroes stepped forward to volunteer for army service, but they were not accepted as soldiers. The Union needed the strength and support of the four border states, where many of the people were slave owners. If Negroes served as soldiers in the Union Army, it was felt that the border states, too, might secede. Negroes were barred from the army, and some slaves were even returned to their masters.

Negro volunteers were determined to have some part in the war effort. For the first year and a half of the war, they served as workers. Some cooked for the troops; others were teamsters who cared for the horses. There were Negro blacksmiths and dock workers. Many served as laborers, building fortifications and other necessary projects. Through their service, they helped the Union Army.

In the Confederate states, Negroes helped the Confederate Army. Many of the slaves continued working on the plantations. Through their work, they supplied the necessary food and clothing for the soldiers. Some slaves followed their masters into the army where they worked as bodyguards and personal servants. Free Negroes in the South worked in labor battalions where they built bridges and drove supply wagons. Some free Negroes fought as soldiers.

The South lost many slaves as the Union forces pushed deeper into Confederate territory. Runaways by the hundreds left their plantations and followed Union troops in a bid for freedom. The hordes of slave families became a problem for Union generals who had no official instructions for their care. Some generals tried to return the runaways to their owners, but this practice was soon stopped. It seemed strange to the Union generals to return slaves to Confederate planters, since the work of the slaves would hurt the Union cause.

Negroes as Contraband

General Benjamin Butler found one solution to the runaway problem. He was the commander of Fortress Monroe in Virginia. One day in May 1861, he was visited by a Confederate officer who demanded the return of three runaway slaves. General Butler pointed out that Virginia claimed to have withdrawn from the Union. He also stated that the slaves would be used against the Union forces if they were returned. So they would be kept as contrabands, or confiscated articles of war.

Whatever term they were called, even greater numbers of slaves fled to Union lines and freedom. They called Fortress Monroe the

*Negroes freed by the Emancipation Proclamation struggle toward
a Union Army camp.*

"freedom fort." They flocked to other Union strongholds, also. Each commanding officer worked out his own way of providing for the contrabands. Some runaways worked in labor groups with the Union Army as scouts, guides, spies, and cooks. There were others who were given abandoned land and were set to work raising much-needed food crops. Some generals had the ex-slaves build rough shelters for themselves and their families. It was at one of these contraband camps that Harriet Tubman gave unselfish service. She worked with the people and set up training centers where the runaways could learn new skills. Harriet Tubman later reported that the men at her camp fished, and worked as laborers for the army. Women washed, cooked, and sewed. Some worked as nurses in the overcrowded hospitals.

Negroes as Soldiers and Sailors

At the beginning of the war, there were high hopes that the Union armies would quickly overcome the Confederate forces. All of the advantages seemed overwhelmingly on the side of the North. There were twenty-three Union states to eleven Confederate states. The North had a much larger population and a greater number of factories that could manufacture war supplies. Hopes for a short war seemed to be well founded. But those hopes soon faded as the South fought a surprisingly effective war. During the first two years of the war, victory after victory was won by the Confederates. These men were fighting largely on home territory, and their generals were well trained in military tactics. As the war lasted longer and longer, the Union armies felt a sharp need for more manpower. Generals who did not have enough troops considered using Negroes, who were already serving in the army but not fighting. A Federal Law, of July 1862, authorized the enlistment of Negroes into the Union forces. General Butler recruited the first regiment of Negro volunteers as soldiers in the Union Army. In September 1862, the First Regiment of the New Orleans Native Guards, a segregated regiment, was formed. These were the first Negro soldiers who were officially mustered into the Union Army. More were mustered in 1863.

Frederick Douglass, the great abolitionist, called upon the free Negroes of the North to volunteer. In a recruiting paper, *Men of Color, To Arms!* he wrote,

> The day dawns; the morning star is bright
> on the horizon! The iron gate of our
> prison stands half-open. One gallant rush
> from the North will fling it wide open,
> while four million of our brothers and
> sisters shall march out into liberty. . . .
> This is our golden opportunity. Let us
> accept it. . . . Let us win for ourselves
> the gratitude of our country, and the best
> blessings of our posterity through all time.[1]

The golden opportunity spoken of by Frederick Douglass was accepted. His own two sons volunteered for service, as did thousands of other Negroes. By the end of the war, about 180,000 Negroes had fought in the Union Army. There were 30,000 others who served in the Union Navy.

The courage of Negro troops in the Union Army equaled the courage of other soldiers. One example of determination was shown by Anselmas Plancianois, a flag bearer who took part in the attack on Fort Hudson in Mississippi. Just before the battle, Plancianois said to his commanding officer, "Colonel, I will bring these colors to you in honor or report to God the reason why!" [2] During the furious charge of battle, Plancianois did indeed lose his life. As he fell, the flag was snatched from his hand by another soldier who wanted the honor of carrying it forward. Before the battle was over, six men had died protecting and defending the flag.

Some Negroes also served as officers in the Union Army. The first of the Negro officers was Major Martin R. Delany, a doctor who had received his training at Harvard Medical School. An-

---

[1] Frederick Douglass, *The Life and Times of Frederick Douglass,* revised (New York: Collier Books, 1962), p. 341.
[2] Benjamin Quarles, *The Negro in the Civil War* (Boston: Little, Brown and Company, 1953), p. 214.

other courageous Negro officer was Captain André Cailloux, who led the attack on Fort Hudson. Like Anselmas Plancianois, Captain Cailloux was killed in battle. Approximately one hundred Negroes were commissioned as officers in the Union Army during the Civil War. During this war, twenty-one Congressional Medals of Honor were awarded to Negroes.

Robert Smalls.   One thrilling story of the war was that of Robert Smalls, who gained his own freedom and helped the Union cause at the same time. Born a slave in South Carolina, Robert Smalls was allowed to learn to read and write. He lived in Charleston, loved the sea, and worked on freighters in the Charleston harbor. Because of his sailing experience, he knew all of the shoals and dangers of the harbor.

When the Civil War broke out, Robert Smalls was forced to serve with the Confederate Navy. He was a deck hand on the Confederate ship *Planter*. The crew of this ship was made up of Negroes, most of whom were slaves. Only the officers were white. Robert Smalls noticed that from time to time the officers of the *Planter* went ashore and spent the entire night away from the ship. He and the other crewmen worked out a daring plan. They would wait for an evening when they were again left alone on the ship. Then they would sail the vessel through Charleston harbor to the Union Navy, which was stationed on the outskirts of the harbor. They would turn the ship over to the Union Navy, and they themselves would be free.

There were dangers, of course. Fort Sumter, now in the hands of the Confederates, might fire upon the ship and destroy it. Or the ship might run aground on dangerous shoals in the darkness of night. The men all knew that if their mission failed, they faced certain death. But they were determined to try.

When the officers left the *Planter* for a night of relaxation ashore, Smalls started to put the plan into action. The crew waited until about three o'clock in the morning before starting. The wives and children of some of the men came aboard and joined the trip to freedom. Then they set sail. Would the guards at Fort Sumter

Robert Smalls stands behind the three
who helped him seize a Confederate ship, the Planter, *below.*

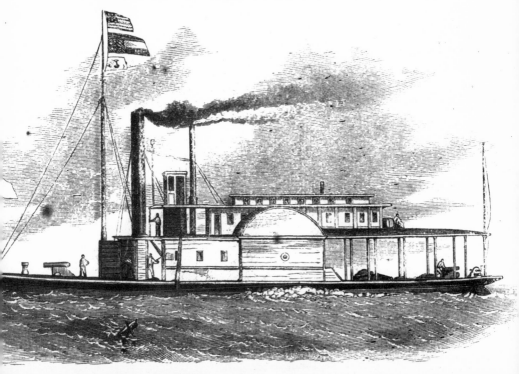

think that this was a routine run by the *Planter,* or would the ship become a target for the ready cannons? Robert Smalls ordered the Confederate flag to be flown high on the mast. He wore the captain's huge straw hat and stood on deck where his silhouette would be mistaken for the captain's, under cover of darkness. He gave the correct signals to each of the sentries as the ship slipped by Fort Sumter. When the Union Navy came into sight, down came the Confederate flag to be replaced by a white flag of truce. The *Planter* was turned over to the Union Navy and was used by the North until the end of the war.

What happened to Robert Smalls? He was given his freedom and served as a pilot in the Union Navy. At one time when the *Planter* was under heavy Confederate attack, another pilot deserted the ship. Robert Smalls took command of the vessel and brought it to safety. For this heroic deed, he was promoted to captain. He remained in charge of the *Planter* until the close of the war. Captain Smalls' military career ended when the Civil War was over, but he continued to serve his country. He later served in both the House of Representatives and the Senate in the state of South Carolina. In 1875, he was elected to the United States House of Representatives.

Important Documents

The Civil War was fought from April, 1861, to April, 1865. During these years of crisis, the country poured all of its strength into the winning of the war and the reuniting of the country. The national government had great responsibility in making decisions that would help the war effort and strengthen the country after the war. Two important documents made their appearance during the war years. They were the Emancipation Proclamation and the Thirteenth Amendment to the Constitution.

An idealized view of a reading of the Emancipation Proclamation.

The Emancipation Proclamation—January 1, 1863

In 1862, experts realized that the war would be a long, drawn-out effort. Congress approved the idea of taking northern Negroes into the armed services. President Lincoln decided to free the southern slaves in order to lessen the help the slaves were giving to their Confederate masters and to encourage them to join the Union rather than the Confederate forces. President Lincoln issued a preliminary draft of the Emancipation Act in September 1862. It stated that the slaves of persons in states, or even parts of states, that were rebelling against the Union would be free. Slaves in the loyal border states were not affected by it. The Proclamation went into effect on January 1, 1863.

This important document did not end slavery. It was generally ignored in the South, though a number of southern slaves escaped

to the North to freedom. The Proclamation did affect the course of the war. For the first time, the abolition of slavery became one of the purposes of the Civil War. The official stand against slavery gained the approval of many European countries. England, particularly, favored the North in the war after the Emancipation Proclamation.

After the proclamation, the enlistment of Negro troops into the Union Army went into quick effect. In the South, even greater numbers of slaves deserted the plantations and flocked to Union forces. The Confederate states lost much of their labor force. Supplies of food and clothing, formerly produced by slaves, were even harder to obtain. Wheat became so scarce, for example, that the price of flour rose to a hundred dollars a barrel. People in the South became accustomed to using ground acorns for flour and roasted, ground-up sweet potatoes as a substitute for coffee. Perhaps the most important result of the Emancipation Proclamation was the fact that it gave hope for genuine freedom to almost four million Negroes in the South.

The Thirteenth Amendment—December, 1865

The abolition of slavery throughout the United States was finally accomplished by the Thirteenth Amendment to the Constitution. This amendment states that slavery shall not exist in any part of the United States or in any territory governed by the United States. In addition, the amendment grants to Congress the power to pass appropriate laws to enforce the abolition of slavery. The Thirteenth Amendment went into effect on December 18, 1865. The long yearning for freedom was satisfied.

The Freedmen

Freedom came suddenly into the lives of most of the slaves. For some individuals who fled to contraband camps during the war years, freedom came as a result of their own efforts. Others remained on plantations until the Thirteenth Amendment went into effect. With emancipation came a complete change from the former way of living. While glorying in being their own masters, freedmen suddenly found that they had no shelter, no work, no food. They had no tools for any occupation; they had no land to plant in food crops. Many of the freedmen had had no chance for education and little training in helping themselves. The familiar pattern of plantation life had ended so abruptly that nothing had been planned to take its place. There followed a period of great confusion, a time of suffering and need. Immediate help was necessary to supply food, shelter, clothing, medicine, and educational training for the freedmen.

Help was not long in coming. Even during the early war years, private relief societies in northern cities collected money, medicine, tools, and clothing for the aid of the freedmen. One of the organizations which gave much help was the American Missionary Association. This group sent teachers and missionaries into the South to start schools and churches in which the freedmen would be given training. One of the first schools was established in 1861, in the city of Hampton, Virginia. Its teacher was Mrs. Mary Peake, a free Negro.

Freedmen were eager to attend the schools that were being opened. Teachers found their classrooms filled with pupils of all ages, as young and old alike pored over their letters. When a new school opened in the town of New Bern, North Carolina, the teacher was amazed to see six hundred Negro pupils coming for classes the very first night. During the day, this school taught poor white pupils who had no other chance for education.

The Freedmen's Bureau

In 1865, the government formed a special organization to help solve the distress of the freedmen. The organization was named the Bureau of Refugees, Freedmen and Abandoned Lands; but it was generally called the Freedmen's Bureau. A great deal of work faced the Freedmen's Bureau. Problems that needed immediate attention were the relief of hunger, the construction of shelters, and the care of the sick. In addition, there were other, long-range problems that the Bureau hoped to solve by training

On pages 106 and 107:
Children and adults study at a freedman's school, Mississippi.

the freedmen to help themselves. Because education was important for free men, many schools were needed. Because free men
needed to earn a living, job training was important and work had
to be found. Because the health of the free men had to be protected, hospitals were needed. The Freedmen's Bureau also served
as a guardian of justice whenever disputes arose between the freedmen and their former masters.

The Freedmen's Bureau gave help in all of these areas of need.
Its greatest accomplishment was in the field of education. During
the seven years it operated from 1865 to 1872, this organization
established more than four thousand schools throughout the
South. Almost 250,000 Negro students, both young and old,
attended classes for the first time in their lives. After being denied
the chance to learn as slaves, the freedmen regarded education
as a golden key to self-improvement. Poor white families, who
had had little chance for education, also sent their children to
the schools.

Some of the schools supported by the Freedmen's Bureau became colleges organized mainly for Negro students. Fisk University in Tennessee, Hampton Institute in Virginia, Atlanta University in Georgia, Morehouse College in Georgia, and Howard
University in Washington, D.C., were all started with the help of
the Bureau. A brief description of three of the colleges will show
the importance of education to the freedmen.

Fisk University.   This famous university, located in Nashville,
Tennessee, did not start as a college. Founded in 1865, it first
provided education from the primary grades up. Its first building
was makeshift; the classes met in an abandoned army hospital.
From the beginning, it was overcrowded; an average of over a
thousand pupils attended every day. When more schools for
young pupils were built in Nashville, Fisk gradually became a
college. It specialized in the training of teachers and ministers
who, in turn, would teach and help others. Teachers trained at
Fisk brought educational opportunities to thousands of boys and
girls throughout the South.

At one time, it was feared that lack of money would cause Fisk University to close. The treasurer of the college, George White, thought of an unusual plan to raise money. He had noticed that the concerts given by the college choir in Nashville were well attended. Mr. White planned to take part of the choir on a concert tour through large cities in the North. The students would raise money for the college by their singing. A small group of nine, five girls and four boys, made the first tour. In one of their songs, they sang of 1865 as the year of freedom, the year of jubilee. From the words of this song, they got their name, the Jubilee Singers from Fisk University.

The first concert was not an overwhelming success. They raised not quite fifty dollars. Since this concert was given at the time of the great Chicago fire, the Jubilee Singers donated the entire amount to the Chicago Relief Fund. The tour became more successful as the group sang its way from city to city. By the end of 1874, they had raised about forty thousand dollars. A later tour in Europe was highly successful. Besides raising additional funds for the university, the Fisk Jubilee Singers were the first Negro musicians to gain international fame.

Hampton Institute. Hampton Institute in Virginia is another important university that was started with the help of the Freedmen's Bureau. Opened in 1868, Hampton Institute was an industrial high school for many years.

The school was first headed by General Samuel Armstrong, a white commander of Negro troops during the Civil War. General Armstrong felt that the freedmen's greatest need was to learn the skills necessary for earning a living. In order to develop these skills, the school emphasized training in farming methods and trades. Pupils who attended Hampton Institute were given the chance to earn part of their way by working for the school. Habits of self-help and thrift were encouraged in this way.

General Armstrong believed that education was the most important way to give lasting help to the freedmen. He had a dream for his school which he expressed by saying:

Students at Hampton Institute practice mechanical drawing.

I will found a school to educate teachers for this race. I will begin in a humble way a more patriotic, more difficult work than fighting for my country. I will open the door for the people, whom I dearly love, into intelligence, self-control, manhood and womanhood, and send my pupils all over this southern land to be centers of light and love, examples of diligence and loyalty to the noblest motives.[3]

General Armstrong's dream came true. Graduates of Hampton helped spread learning throughout the South. Today Hampton Institute continues to educate young people for many different professions.

[3] Edwin Embree, *Brown Americans* (New York: Viking Press, 1943), pp. 75–76.

Howard University. Howard University, with the help of the Freedmen's Bureau, was opened in Washington, D.C., in 1867. This university differed from the others in that all students were welcome. Negro and white were admitted, young and old, married and single. Students from the North, the South, and the West came to study at Howard. Besides the regular college courses, Howard University also had an excellent Medical College. Freedmen's Hospital was established, and the work of the hospital was closely related to the work of the university. Medical students from Howard trained as interns and doctors at Freedmen's Hospital. Howard University also developed an outstanding College of Law.

In 1926, a Negro educator and minister was appointed president of Howard University. He was one of the first Negro college presidents in our country. Mordecai Johnson was only thirty-six years old when he came to the university as its leader, and he was to remain 34 years as president. He had studied at Morehouse College, another institution started with help from the Freedmen's Bureau. Later, he attended the University of Chicago and then Harvard University where he earned a Master's degree. He obtained a Doctor's degree from Gammon Theological Seminary. After this thorough preparation, he became a successful minister in Charleston, West Virginia.

Mordecai Johnson was equally interested in education. He had been a professor at Morehouse College for a number of years. When he came to Howard University as president, he brought about many improvements in the college. By 1956, the Medical College of Howard University was recognized throughout the country for its high standards. At that time, almost one half of all Negro doctors and dentists in the United States received their training at the Howard University Medical College. The Law College also became outstanding. Here, approximately one fourth of the country's Negro lawyers were trained. Under the leadership of Dr. Mordecai Johnson, Howard University added Schools of Graduate Study and Social Work. The university has continued to grow in size and to advance in standards of achievement.

Negro delegates to the United States Senate and House of Representatives elected during the reconstruction period. From the left: Hiram Revels, Senator from Mississippi and Representatives Benjamin Turner from Alabama, Robert de Large from South Carolina, Josiah Walls from Florida, Jefferson Long from Georgia, and Joseph Rainy and R. B. Elliot from South Carolina.

Reconstruction Days

The Civil War ended in 1865 with the surrender of the Confederate forces. This tragic war settled two questions which had divided the country. It proved that the nation itself was more powerful than any one state or any group of states, and it brought an end to slavery.

After the war, there were many problems that needed immediate attention. The South had suffered great losses, since most of the battles had been fought on southern territory. Cities and towns lay in ruins. Homes had been burned and plantations destroyed. Transportation was difficult because roads and railroads had been wrecked. Most of the southerners had lost their fortunes, large or small, in the war effort. They had used their money to buy Confederate war bonds. This money was forever lost. Gone, too, was the money that had been used to buy slaves before the war. The plantation system had come to a final end. Emancipation had brought freedom to the slave. It had brought loss of wealth to his master. One of the big problems was the rebuilding of the South.

Another important problem centered around the eleven Confederate states which had broken away from the Union. Now that the war was over, what plans should be made to restore these states to their place in the Union? What plans would be needed to reunite the two sections of the nation? Each of the Confederate states needed to reorganize its own state government. Many of the men who had been political leaders before the Civil War had fought against the Union in the war years. Should these men be allowed to hold political office? Answers to these questions had to be found before northerners and southerners would feel at ease with each other.

The care of the freedmen was another overwhelming problem, one already tackled by the Freedmen's Bureau. Of far greater importance, however, were decisions about the place of the freedmen in the life of the country. By the Thirteenth Amendment, slaves had been granted freedom. Should the federal government insist that they be granted all the privileges of citizenship as well?

Reconstruction

During the period of American history spanning the years 1865 to 1877 and known as *reconstruction,* the nation worked to reunite itself. It was a time of crisis and confusion which brought radical changes to the South, including the granting of the privileges of citizenship to the freedmen. It was a period of bitterness for the defeated Confederates.

Reconstruction Plans of the Presidents

Even while the war was being fought, President Lincoln had made plans for the reuniting of the nation. Hoping this could be accomplished smoothly, he wished the country to work for peace rather than to remember the bitterness of war. The terms of his reconstruction plan were lenient toward the defeated Confederacy, but he would not live to see a smooth reconstruction. His tragic assassination put the leadership of the country into the hands of Andrew Johnson.

President Johnson's reconstruction plan was no harsher than

Lincoln's. Confederate soldiers who had fought against the Union were required simply to pledge their loyalty to the United States. By this act, they were pardoned and were permitted once more to vote and to hold political power. Within a few months, all the former Confederate states except Texas had adopted new constitutions and organized new governments. But little was said about the right of the freedmen to vote. President Johnson felt that each state should work out this problem separately and that the national government should not make a rule for all the states to follow.

In the meantime the Confederate states were trying to make laws to deal with the change in their economic system. They passed laws concerning the newly freed slaves. Some of the laws listed certain jobs that Negroes could hold; other jobs were closed by law to the freedmen. In some states, Negroes were prohibited from owning property. Freedmen without jobs were considered vagrants and could be arrested. Their sentences would be either a fine or a certain period of labor. These and other such laws restricting the ex-slaves were called Black Codes. Instead of giving opportunities to Negroes, the Black Codes took them away. Because of the harsh laws, Negroes were forced to remain in the position of servants, with little opportunity to take a free and active part in community life. All of these laws were made by officials who had been elected by white voters only. Negroes were not allowed to vote.

Reconstruction Plans of Congress

Congress did not approve of President Johnson's reconstruction plan. Many Congressmen felt that Negroes should be allowed to vote; Negro votes would elect officials who would protect Negro freedom. These Congressmen criticized the Black Codes as examples of poor laws that blocked freedom for the ex-slaves.

Eventually, Congress passed a series of laws that dealt with reconstruction. These laws included the Reconstruction Act of 1867, the Fourteenth Amendment to the Constitution, drafted in 1866 and adopted in 1868, and the Fifteenth Amendment of

1870. Each of the national laws would be enforced in every state of the Union. Through these laws the national government led the way in granting the duties and privileges of citizenship to freedmen.

Fourteenth Amendment to the Constitution. The Fourteenth Amendment to the Constitution made the Negroes of the United States citizens. It states, "All persons born or naturalized in the United States . . . are citizens of the United States and of any state wherein they reside."

To make sure that all states would recognize Negroes as citizens, Congress ruled that the Confederate states must agree to the terms of the Fourteenth Amendment. Tennessee was the only former Confederate state to ratify the amendment. The ten other states refused to do so and remained outside the Union.

Reconstruction Act. Through the Reconstruction Act, Congress set up a system of temporary government for the ten Confederate states that had rejected the Fourteenth Amendment.

One of the important parts of the Reconstruction Act was concerned with voting. It permitted freedmen to vote and to hold political office. Before white citizens could vote, they were required to take an oath of allegiance to the United States, generally called the "ironclad oath." Men who took the oath swore that they had never voluntarily borne arms against the United States nor had held any office under the Confederacy. Men who had been officials in the Confederacy were not allowed to vote or to hold political office. Many of these men had been the political leaders of the South before the Civil War. All in all, about 200,000 ex-Confederates lost their right to vote. When these men lost their right to vote, the white voters of the South lost their majority.

After the Reconstruction Act, approximately 1,360,000 men registered as voters in the ten Confederate states that had refused to ratify the Fourteenth Amendment. Of these 660,000 were whites who took the oath of allegiance; 700,000 were Negroes who were voting for the first time in their lives.

"THE FIRST VOTE."—Drawn by A. R. Waud.—[See Next Page.]

Freed Negroes casting their first ballots as citizens.

Voting was not the only new political experience for the freed-man in the South. For the first time, he, too, could be elected to office. If elected, a freedman could take an active part in making laws and in writing constitutions for his state.

Federal troops were sent into the Confederate states to make sure that the Reconstruction Act was obeyed. The power of the national government was upheld by a military force.

Fifteenth Amendment to the Constitution—1870.   The Fifteenth Amendment guaranteed to all male citizens, including Negroes, an equal right to vote. It states that, "The right of citizens of the United States to vote shall not be denied or abridged . . . on ac-count of race, color, or previous condition of servitude." The amendment was then sent to the states to be approved. By 1870, the Fifteenth Amendment was ratified, and all the Confederate states had been restored to the Union.

Reconstruction Government

The South of 1870 had undergone many changes. Federal troops remained in the region to protect the rights of the freedmen. Former political leaders, deprived of their voting privileges, were merely spectators at elections. They watched both Negro and white citizens who were loyal to the Union use the ballots. They stood by, also, when Negroes were elected to political offices. Ex-Confederates who had been slaveholders bitterly resented the thought of Negroes filling positions of political power. Many felt that ex-slaves had had neither the training nor the experience to understand these responsibilities. They predicted that the new state governments would fail.

Negroes in Government

One important task faced by each Confederate state was to write a new state constitution. The people who were to write the new constitutions were chosen by elections and were sent as dele-gates to a special meeting called a constitutional convention.

Some of the Negro delegates to these constitutional conventions had been slaves. Others had been born free and were used to responsibilities. There were some among the Negro leaders who had once lived in the South but had fled north to find freedom. Some of these men were well educated; some had served well with the Union Army. When the need for leadership arose in the South, they returned and took an active part in political affairs. Because of their experience and training, they were capable leaders. Robert Elliott, for example, who served as a delegate to the South Carolina convention, had studied in schools in Boston and in London. His academic record at Eton in England had been outstanding; and he could read French, Spanish, German, and Latin. P. B. S. Pinchback of Louisiana had been a captain of the Louisiana Native Guards during the Civil War. Still another political leader was Francis L. Cardozo, who had received his education at the University of Glasgow in Scotland. Some Negro delegates had been ministers; a few had been school teachers or lawyers. Some had worked with the Freedmen's Bureau. From different backgrounds of experience and education, Negro and white delegates met to set up new governments for the Confederate states. Many of these delegates went on to serve in important state and national offices.

Negroes in State Governments.   The delegates to the constitutional conventions worked together to write new constitutions. These new constitutions promised more opportunity to all citizens—rich or poor, white or Negro. For the first time in the South, state constitutions provided for free public schools for all children. It was now possible for children of poor white families, as well as Negroes, to receive the advantage of education. The new constitutions also made it easier for citizens to vote and to hold political office. For years, citizens who voted had been required to own a certain amount of property. The privilege of voting was, in this way, kept under the control of the richer people. The new constitutions removed this property requirement and granted to all male citizens the right to vote, to serve on

juries, and to hold political office. Harsh punishments were also
abolished by some state constitutions. Imprisonment for debt,
branding, the whipping post, and the stocks were all declared
illegal. In addition, the constitutions provided the framework for
the new state governments.

Negroes were elected to many positions in the state governments. They served as sheriffs, state senators and representatives,
and judges. South Carolina, Mississippi, and Louisiana elected
Negro lieutenant-governors. Within each Confederate state, Negro
and white elected officials worked together to try to solve some
of the problems of the South.

Negroes in the National Government.   Negroes took an active
part in the national government, too. During the reconstruction
years, twenty-two were elected to the United States Congress; two
of these men served in the Senate.

Hiram R. Revels was the first Negro to be elected to the Senate.
He was born free in North Carolina in 1822. While still young,
he moved to Ohio where he had a better chance for getting an
education. Hiram Revels studied in a Quaker school in Ohio and
then attended Knox College in Illinois. He became a successful
minister in the African Methodist Episcopal Church and then
taught school for a year. During the Civil War years, he worked
in the contraband camps, starting schools, organizing churches,
and helping the homeless Negro refugees who followed the Union
armies. He finally made his home in Mississippi. Here he gained
political experience by serving as state senator before going on
to represent Mississippi as a United States Senator between 1870
and 1871. He took over the Senate seat formerly held by the
Confederate, Jefferson Davis.

The second Negro Senator was also elected from Mississippi.
Blanche Bruce had been born a slave in Virginia but had escaped
to the North. Realizing the importance of education, he attended
Oberlin College in Ohio. At the end of the Civil War, he went
to Mississippi to live. He was elected to serve in the United States
Senate from 1875 to 1881.

The Negroes who were elected to the United States House of Representatives were, for the most part, well educated and experienced in political service. South Carolina sent the largest number of Negro Representatives; eight Negroes from this state served in Washington. Robert Smalls, the Civil War hero, and Robert Elliott, a Representative to the South Carolina State Legislature, were both sent by South Carolina to the nation's capital. Twelve other Negro Representatives were sent from seven different states. Four were elected from North Carolina; three from Alabama; and one each from the states of Florida, Georgia, Louisiana, Mississippi, and Virginia. Thirteen of these men had been born into slavery, and ten of them had had college training.

Carpetbaggers and Scalawags

Reconstruction governments became firmly established in the South, despite the bitter objections of the wealthy planters who had once been the political leaders. The planters could do little to change the new situation for two reasons. First, federal troops remained in the South to enforce the new laws. Second, under the terms of the Reconstruction Act, officials of the defeated Confederacy were not permitted to vote. The very persons who had once had the greatest amount of political experience were not allowed to take part in the government.

White southerners resented two groups of men other than the Negroes who took part in the reconstruction governments. They were the carpetbaggers and the scalawags. The term carpetbaggers was given to all northerners who worked in the South during the reconstruction years. The strange name reflected the low opinion that southerners had of them. It was said that they packed everything they owned into one old-fashioned traveling bag made of cheap carpeting, a "carpetbag." They were looked upon as intruders who came from another region to seek political power. The insulting name of carpetbagger was even given to northern missionaries and school teachers who worked unselfishly to help the freedmen. Those southerners who could not vote or make laws felt it was unfair for northerners to be active in their state governments.

Scalawags were also despised by many of the ex-planters. This term was given to white southerners who had opposed secession during the war years and who now cooperated with reconstruction policies. Since the scalawags carried out reconstruction orders, they were considered by ex-Confederates to be traitors to the southern cause.

Made up largely of Negroes, carpetbaggers, and scalawags, the new governments were called carpetbag governments. Much has been written about the inefficiency and dishonesty of reconstruction governments. Bitter and violent criticisms were made by white southerners who feared Negro power and northern intervention. Refusing to believe that any good could be accomplished by reconstruction lawmakers, many ex-Confederates found fault with the new state constitutions. In some instances, mistakes actually had been made. Men who were not experienced in making laws sometimes made poor laws. Men who were not used to political power sometimes misused their power. There were also cases where some officials deliberately stole public funds to make their own fortunes. This unfortunate situation did not exist only in the South. During the same years, there were dishonest public officials in the northern states, as well. In the confusion that followed the Civil War, examples of bad government could be found in all parts of our country. However, the majority of political leaders were honest. A modern historian, Professor C. Vann Woodward, has made a careful study of the work of Negro public officials. In describing them, he stated: "One is more impressed with the success that a people of such meager resources and limited experience enjoyed in producing the number of sober, honest, and capable leaders and public servants they did." Many of the laws passed by the carpetbag governments were just and fair. Progress in free education was a real step forward. Laws about public education remained in common use for years after the reconstruction period had ended.

The Weakening of the Reconstruction Government

Reconstruction gradually came to an end in the late 1870's. Several events occurred that put political power back into the hands of the former southern leaders. How did this happen? First, the Negroes were discouraged from voting. When they lost their voting privileges, they no longer had the chance to take an active part in making laws. Then, gradually, a greater number of ex-Confederates gained the right to vote. By the beginning of 1869, President Johnson had pardoned almost all former Confederates. With pardon had come the privileges of voting and holding political office. As more of these men came into power, there was a sharp reversal of many of the laws that had given political freedom to Negroes. Finally, in the late 1870's, the remaining federal troops were withdrawn from the South. The pro-slavery leaders of the ex-Confederate states were freer to run their states more as they had before the war.

Ku Klux Klan.   Fear, rather than law, was used to keep Negroes from voting. In the late 1860's, secret organizations were formed to weaken carpetbag governments and to frighten Negroes from voting. The most notorious of these organizations was the Ku Klux Klan, which was organized in Pulaski, Tennessee, in 1865. Members of the Klan were sworn to secrecy. When they rode through the countryside at night, Klansmen were disguised by long robes with hoods. The robes served a purpose, for some men would do things, while disguised, that they would not have the courage to do openly. Originally the Ku Klux Klan planned to take advantage of the fears and superstitions of the ex-slaves. A sudden and ghostlike appearance in the middle of the night and a solemn warning against voting were the first activities of the Klansmen. When these tactics declined in effectiveness, their actions became more extreme and uncontrolled. The warnings were followed by terror tactics, and Klansmen often used threats, force, and even acts of violence to spread greater fear. The vio-

Some early disguises of Ku Klux Klan members.

lence and lawless actions of the Klan disturbed a number of southern leaders who tried to disband the organization, but the Klan was too strong for them. In 1871, Congress took action against the Ku Klux Klan to lessen its activities but not before it had accomplished its purpose. Thousands of Negroes were kept from voting through fear and violence.

Amnesty Act, 1872.   In 1872, Congress passed the Amnesty Act. *Amnesty* means pardon, and this act granted official pardon to almost all of the former Confederate leaders who had not been pardoned up to this time. After the Amnesty Act, fewer than five hundred individuals were still denied the right to vote and hold political office.

Withdrawal of Federal Troops. The official end of the reconstruction period came in 1877, when federal troops were ordered from the South by President Rutherford Hayes. During the stormy reconstruction years, the army had given support to the new governments. Throughout that period, the original number of troops had gradually been reduced, and by 1877 there were relatively few soldiers in the South. Their withdrawal removed the last bit of support from the weakened carpetbag governments. Reconstruction was dead. It had been a period of enforced radical change, a time of misunderstanding and hatred. For Negroes and poor whites, it had been a beginning of political participation. After the end of the reconstruction period, the leaders stopped trying to bring greater equality to all citizens.

Reaction Against Reconstruction Rule

Throughout the 1870's and 1880's, there were few determined efforts to weaken the Negro's freedom. For a while, it seemed possible that the South would continue to recognize the Negro's rights as a citizen. In 1885, for example, a Negro newspaperman from Boston traveled to South Carolina. Expecting to experience some discrimination, he was pleasantly surprised to find a high degree of equality. In reporting to his newspaper, he wrote: "Thus far I have found traveling [in Virginia and the Carolinas] more pleasant than in some parts of New England." [1]

Starting in the 1890's, the picture began to change. Reactions against full citizenship for the Negro hardened, and racial discrimination spread. Through laws and customs which strengthened discrimination, the Negro was forced back into an inferior position in the community.

By 1900, southern Negroes were living under three overwhelming handicaps. In an unofficial but nevertheless real way, they had lost their right to vote and take part in making laws.

[1] Hubert Humphrey, editor, *School Desegregation: Documents and Commentaries* (New York: Thomas Y. Crowell Company, 1964), p. 95.

Job opportunities were limited, and most Negroes lived in conditions of grinding poverty. The third handicap was that of racial segregation. These conditions provided little chance for Negroes to improve their lot in the future. Today, leaders of our nation are still working to improve this situation and the accumulated results of it.

Limitation of the Negro Vote

To remove the Negro from the political power he had gained during reconstruction, political leaders did what they could to take away his right to vote. They could not act directly since they had to obey the Fifteenth Amendment. This amendment stated that the right of citizens to vote could not be denied "on account of race, color, or previous condition of servitude." Clearly, any restrictions on voting would have to be based on conditions other than race.

State laws, which listed definite requirements for voting, were passed. In some states, only property owners were permitted to vote. Some states passed poll taxes which voters were required to pay. A poll tax was a certain amount of money which each voter had to pay, usually six months before an election. In addition to paying the tax for the year of the election, the individual was also required to pay all the back taxes for every year since he had come of age. Persons who could not afford the poll tax were not allowed to vote. Both the property requirement and poll tax kept thousands of Negroes from voting. These requirements also made it impossible for thousands of poor whites to use the ballot.

In an effort to reduce the Negro vote without limiting the votes of poor whites, lawmakers made different laws. In some states, voters were required to take a literacy test. The object of the test was to discover whether the voter could understand the topics on which he was to vote. Each individual had to pass the test to the satisfaction of an election official. This official had the final authority to reject the voter or to permit him to vote. In many cases, there were different literacy requirements for Negroes and whites. This test became a legal barrier that few Negroes could overcome.

Even well-educated Negroes—ministers, lawyers, and school teachers—failed to pass the test to the satisfaction of certain officials.

In 1898, Louisiana added still another restriction to the Negro vote. A law containing the well-known "grandfather clause" was enacted. According to this law, the right to vote without meeting certain qualifications was given to all male citizens *whose father or grandfather had voted on January 1, 1867*. Since no Negro, slave or freedman, had voted in 1867, this law meant that only Negroes had to conform to certain conditions before voting. Usually they were required to pass a difficult literacy test or to meet a property requirement. White voters did not face the same requirements. Since their ancestors had been eligible to vote in 1867, they could vote freely even though some were poorly educated or had no property. Laws which included grandfather clauses were effective in blocking the Negro vote. Several states passed laws with grandfather clauses. These laws were enforced until 1915, when the Supreme Court of the United States ruled that they were unconstitutional.

Beginnings of Racial Segregation

Jim Crow was the name given at first to racial segregation. The term was originally heard on the stage. Thomas Rice, a minstrel comedian, sang a dialect song and danced to the tune:

> Weel a-bout and turn a-bout
> And do just so.
> Every time I weel a-bout
> I jump Jim Crow.

By the 1850's, Jim Crow was a synonym for racial segregation.

Jim Crow laws started making an appearance in the 1880's. First, the races were separated on public transportation when trains provided different coaches for Negro and white passengers. This was true in the North as well as in the South. Southern street cars had separate coaches for Negro passengers. In time, other laws which separated the races were passed. The South built racially segregated schools, parks, hospitals, and libraries. In the North, hotels, restaurants, and many places of amusement were segregated by custom. Racial segregation was challenged in 1896. The Supreme Court of the United States heard the case of Homer Plessy, a Negro. Plessy asked the Court's ruling on a Louisiana law which stated that Negroes and whites must be separated on trains. In the *Plessy vs. Ferguson* case, the Supreme Court ruled that the law was constitutional. It stated that separation of the two races could be allowed as long as service and accommodations for each were equally good. Known as the "separate-but-equal" clause, this decision ignored the fact that separate facilities were never equal. It led the way for many additional laws which promoted racial segregation. It was responsible for allowing legal separation, which usually produces discrimination.

In the South, the pattern of segregation became particularly rigid. Understanding and communication between the races were

Discrimination as shown in segregated drinking fountains.

weakened. On both sides, there were feelings of distrust, fear, and hostility which sometimes broke out into violence. Segregation was an expensive system. Great amounts of money would have been needed to provide separate-but-equal schools, libraries, hospitals, and other facilities for the two races. In actual practice, Negro facilities were almost always inferior to those provided for white citizens. In his daily living, the Negro was constantly reminded of his limited opportunities. His children were usually born in a segregated hospital and they attended usually inferior, all-Negro schools. He sat in Jim Crow street cars or drank only from a drinking fountain marked "Colored." When he died, his family buried him in a segregated cemetery.

Georgia tenant farmers living in former slave cabins.

After Reconstruction:
1875—1900

The greatest problem faced by southern Negroes after the Civil War was that of finding work and earning a living. As slaves they had been given food, clothing, and shelter in exchange for their labor. With freedom, however, came the responsibility of earning enough money to provide these things for themselves and their families. The majority of freedmen had been farmers, but they owned no farm land upon which to work. So they returned to the land owners to find work, not as slaves but as wage earners.

The planters of the South had problems about money, also. They had lost much of their wealth in the war effort. Many of the beautiful mansions which had been damaged needed expensive repairs. During the war years, the money crop of cotton had not been grown. Even food crops were scarce, and many of these had been taken by the Union armies. When the planter returned home after the war, he had the task of repairing the home which had been neglected for four years. He also had to find ways of paying the heavy taxes which were levied against his lands. Without ready cash, the planter regarded his land as the only way of earning money. He realized that he needed workers as much as the freedmen needed land upon which to work. Because there was little money to pay cash wages to workers, planters worked out a new system of agriculture. It was tenant farming, or share cropping.

Southern Tenant Farming

Former plantations were divided into smaller tracts of land which were cultivated by the tenant farmer, or worker. The land owners supplied seeds, tools, and a home for the workers. At harvest time, the worker shared the produce with the owner, and each received money for his share of the crop.

Many of the freedmen and poor whites became tenant farmers. Since their yearly wage came at harvest time with the selling of the crops, the tenants often suffered from lack of money in the early months of the year. Without enough savings to buy necessary items during the year, tenants would borrow money to pay for food, clothing, and other necessities. This debt, with interest, would be repaid at harvest when the worker was paid for his year's labor. The pattern of borrowing during the year and paying at harvest time was a vicious cycle which kept most tenant farmers continually in debt. The tenant became bound to the land through debt just as surely as he had been bound to the land through slavery.

Some Negroes tried to improve their living conditions. Some moved away from the South. Others tried to obtain better education and vocational training.

A former slave who regarded himself as the Moses of his people inspired thousands of Negroes to leave the South in the 1870's. Benjamin "Pap" Singleton had escaped from slavery in Tennessee to freedom in Canada, where he lived until after the Emancipation Proclamation. Only then did he return to the South and make a successful living as a cabinetmaker. "Pap" Singleton was deeply concerned about the hardships under which Negroes were living in the 1870's. He was especially disturbed by conditions of poverty, lack of political rights, and the activities of the Ku Klux Klan. Though barely able to write, he was a persuasive speaker. He expressed his belief that Negroes should live together in separate communities. If they lived in all-Negro settlements, then they could work and manage their own affairs without competition from the whites. He praised Kansas as a land of opportunity, a promised land where Negroes could own farms and earn a better living. In 1873, he led a group of three hundred into Kansas. He then returned to the South where he told others of the opportunities waiting in the West. There were many willing listeners. Individuals and groups traveled westward on foot, by horseback, by boat and railroad. The migration movement grew and by 1879, between sixty and eighty thousand Negroes had moved to Kansas. Their lives there were not easy. Most were unprepared for the bitter climate of the state and suffered physical hardships. Many of them obtained land under the Homestead Act and decided to stay in Kansas. A number of the migrants, disappointed and disillusioned, returned to their former homes in the South.

Education

Greater emphasis was placed on education as a way for Negroes to better their situation. From the close of the Civil War to 1915, several wealthy white citizens gave large amounts of money for Negro education in the South. In 1867, George Foster Peabody set up an education fund of two million dollars to establish schools in the poorer districts of the South. In 1882, the John F. Slater Fund was established. From the Anna T. Jeanes Fund, donated in 1905, salaries were paid to Jeanes teachers who worked in small rural Negro schools. The Jeanes teachers taught the adults in the community as well as the children. They emphasized industrial skills for men and boys and homemaking skills for women and girls.

One of the most interesting educational funds was established by Julius Rosenwald in the early 1900's. Rosenwald was interested in encouraging both races of southern communities to work together. His education fund could be used to build schools only under certain conditions. First, a school would be built only in communities where the people wanted one. Second, the people themselves would have to share in the cost of building the school.

One fourth of the cost of the school would be paid by Negro citizens, one fourth by white citizens, and one half by the Rosenwald Fund. In order to share in the cost of a school, Negro and white citizens had to work together and make careful plans. Cooperation between the races was encouraged in this manner. In many communities, this cooperation continued as the races worked together to solve other problems. More than five thousand schools were built throughout the South with aid from the Rosenwald Fund.

Negroes themselves were aware of education as a way to self-improvement. To a greater and greater degree, they became the teachers and educational leaders who opened opportunities to many others.

Booker T. Washington and Tuskegee Institute

On April 5, 1856, a slave boy was born on a small farm in Virginia. Who could have looked at this baby and predicted that, in time, he would become a college president and an influential Negro leader? Whoever dreamed that one day he would eat dinner at the White House with the President of the United States?

As a slave boy, Booker Taliaferro Washington knew the pangs of hunger. But as he grew older, he hungered for more than food. He wanted knowledge; he wanted to know the *how* and *why* of things. When his family moved to West Virginia after the Civil War, nine-year-old Booker T. Washington started to work in the salt mines. As he grew older, he rose at four o'clock in the morning and worked all day. Tired though he was, he still hungered for knowledge. In the evening, he pored over the alphabet and learned to read and write simple words. Then Booker T. Washington heard of a school in Virginia where Negroes could receive an education. He made up his mind to attend that school.

He was just fifteen when he left his home to travel to Hampton Institute. He walked much of the way, earning money for food as he went. At sixteen, he started his studies at Hampton Institute, working in the school sawmill his first year to help pay his way.

Hampton Institute, under the leadership of General Samuel Armstrong, offered education and vocational training to its students. General Armstrong felt that young Negroes needed to learn skills for better jobs that would lift them out of the poverty of tenant farming. Booker T. Washington, also, became convinced that job-training was an important step forward for his race. Very early in his college career, he determined to become a teacher so that he could help others.

After graduation from Hampton, he returned to West Virginia and started his teaching career. There were many eager pupils.

Booker T. Washington

He taught boys and girls during the day and had evening classes for the adults who flocked to his school. After a few years, he returned to Hampton, not as a student but a teacher. Then in 1881, when he was only twenty-five years old, he founded Tuskegee Institute, a new school for Negroes located at Tuskegee, Alabama.

Many men would have been discouraged at the sight of the tumbledown church and small shanty that were the beginnings of Tuskegee Institute. Booker T. Washington was not.

Seeing opportunities in the rickety buildings, he himself led his pupils in many work projects. Together they cleared the land, planted gardens, dug wells, and constructed buildings. The educational program at Tuskegee aimed to educate the hand and heart, as well as the mind. Mental development in academic subjects was stressed. So were moral training and skills in many vocational and technical trades. The school emphasized industrial and agricultural education because Washington felt that Negroes must first get better jobs. Social and political rights were problems that could be worked out later, he thought. He also believed in cooperation between the Negro and Caucasian races. As principal of Tuskegee, he was successful in gaining financial help for his school from wealthy white individuals.

Tuskegee Institute became more than just a school. It was a community center reaching out into the neighborhood to give help to all interested adults. There were special training sessions for ministers, teachers, farmers, and homemakers. In every area, Tuskegee tried to help and inspire individuals toward self-improvement.

Booker T. Washington was the most prominent Negro of the country from 1895 until his death in 1915. He devoted his time and energy to the improvement of Negro life in America.

Dr. George Washington Carver, Teacher and Scientist

This scientist and educator used his talents to help other people. Known as the "Wizard of Tuskegee," George Washington

Carver did work in research that improved farming methods and started new industries in the South.

George Washington Carver was born in a slave cabin in Missouri in 1864. When he was just a few months old, he and his mother were kidnaped. A band of lawless night riders burst into their cabin at night and took them to another state to sell them. Moses Carver, for whom George's mother had worked, was never able to find her again. He did find the sick little baby, and brought him back to the farm and nursed him back to health. George loved the out-of-doors and learned a great deal about plants. Even as a child, he had his own secret garden where he learned how to make plants flourish. His neighbors laughingly called him the plant doctor and asked his advice when their plants needed attention.

George Washington Carver wanted to learn everything he could. Mrs. Carver taught him to read, but George wanted to go to a real school. When he was just ten years old, he left the Carver farm and went to the nearest town where there was a school he could attend. Getting an education was not easy. Young Carver had to work to get enough money to buy food and books. He would go to school for awhile, then stop and earn money for awhile. For some years he wandered through Missouri, Kansas, and Iowa, working and attending school. He worked his way through college. Then he was asked to teach at Tuskegee Institute. He remained there for the rest of his life, teaching and working in science.

Through his work, George Washington Carver was able to help the farmers of the South. The South in the early 1900's still depended heavily on the cotton crop. When cotton was grown in the same fields year after year, the soil lost its richness. Dr. Carver tried to tell the farmers to plant other crops that would restore richness to the soil. He advised them to grow peanuts since this crop would give back to the soil the elements that the cotton took out. The farmers refused to take his advice. Patiently, Dr. Carver decided to show them what could be done. He selected twenty acres of the poorest soil in the region. Then he built up the soil by planting several crops of peanuts, sweet potatoes, and soy beans. After the richness had been restored, he planted vegetables and cotton. At harvest time, the farmers were amazed to see cabbages that were twenty inches across and fine big bolls of cotton. Only then did they have faith in Dr. Carver's advice, and many farmers planted peanuts. So many planted peanuts, however, that there was a great surplus of this crop. There were no buyers for so many peanuts.

Dr. Carver worked in his laboratory to try to find products that could be made from this crop. He worked patiently for many years. During this time, he found over three hundred different products which could be manufactured from the peanut. Among

George Washington Carver and Henry Ford

them were meal, coffee, ink, paper, shaving cream, linoleum, milk, cheese, and soap. He analyzed the sweet potato, also, and discovered many products that could be made from it. As a result of his discoveries, new industries were started in the South. Factories were built, and new jobs were made available for many workers.

Industry

One of the most important developments in the United States in the late 1800's was the rapid growth of industry. People in the North had long depended on manufacturing as a way of earning a living. After the Civil War, many new large factories were built. Complicated machinery was used to produce manufactured goods rapidly and accurately. With the break-up of the plantation system after the war, industry became more important to the people of the South, too. Coal mining, iron and steel production, and the textile industry were all developed in the South.

Growing industry needed men to work in the factories. During the late 1800's, many of the skilled factory workers were immigrants who flocked from Europe to live in the United States. For the most part, Negroes were denied the chance to work in skilled occupations; white workers were given the better jobs. Negroes generally filled the unskilled jobs, which paid the lowest salaries. When opportunity to use talent was given, however, some men developed inventions that were important to the growth of industry.

Negro Inventors

Norbert Rillieux.   Norbert Rillieux was an engineer whose invention was important to the sugar industry. Born a slave in New Orleans in 1806, Norbert was a highly intelligent boy. His master saw that he got an education and later sent the boy to France to attend college there. After completing his college career, Norbert Rillieux remained for a few years to teach in a French school. When he returned to New Orleans, he came as a freedman. His talent as an engineer was recognized, and he was hired to reorganize a large sugar refining plant.

Sugar was an important industry to the lower South. The cane was fed into giant presses that crushed moisture from the stalks. After a slow process of evaporation, sugar was obtained from the juices. Norbert Rillieux invented machinery that greatly improved the method of evaporation. His machine speeded up evaporation and made it possible to extract the sugar at a lower cost. In addition, there was an improvement in the sugar that was refined in this manner. Before Rillieux's machine was used, sugar was coarse and brown. Sugar obtained by the new method was fine and white, much like the sugar that we use today. In time, the machine invented by Norbert Rillieux was used in all tropical lands where sugar cane was grown. This invention was as important to the sugar industry as the cotton gin was to cotton farming. Today, the Rillieux process of evaporation is also used in making condensed milk, soap, gelatin, and glue.

Elijah McCoy.   Elijah McCoy was interested in machinery. He invented a number of devices that made it possible to oil heavy machinery mechanically. Although his parents had been slaves in Kentucky, they had reached Canada by way of the Underground Railroad. Here, Elijah McCoy was born in 1844. As a young man, McCoy spent some time in Scotland where he worked with machinery.

When Elijah McCoy came to Detroit to live, he worked as a fireman on one of the railroads. One of his duties was to lubricate the engines. Hand oiling was slow and tedious. As he went about his work, McCoy thought of ways of doing this important task more efficiently. He invented a lubricating cup which made it possible to oil machines and engines without stopping them. This device is still used on railroads and steamships today. Elijah McCoy worked out other inventions, each having something to do with the lubrication of machinery. Between 1872 and 1920, this inventor was granted fifty-seven patents for different lubricating devices.

Jan Ernest Matzeliger. Jan Matzeliger improved the shoe manufacturing industry. His invention put an end to the tedious handwork that had been necessary in making shoes. Jan Matzeliger was born in Dutch Guiana in 1852. When he came to the United States, he worked as an apprentice to a shoemaker in Philadelphia. After his apprenticeship, he settled in Lynn, Massachusetts, and worked in a shoe factory.

Shoemaking was a highly skilled occupation. Although machinery was used for the sewing of the uppers and for the shaping of the soles, the important task of sewing the uppers to the soles was done by hand. Careful attention had to be given to the shaping of the uppers. The men who did the final stitching were paid high wages for their skill.

Jan Matzeliger had ideas for a machine that would do this complicated work. Using pieces of scrap lumber and scrap iron and old cigar boxes, he worked on his idea at night. Time after time he experienced failure as he worked at the crude machine. Five years went by, and Jan Matzeliger understood why other men who had tried to construct such a machine had failed. But he did not give up. After ten years, he built a machine that could attach the upper to the sole of a shoe as perfectly as men could. Matzeliger's machine turned out four hundred perfect pairs of shoes in one day. Skilled workmen were able to hand stitch between forty and fifty pairs a day. Factories could manufacture many more shoes by using this machine, and shoe exports jumped from one million to eleven million pairs a year.

Jan Matzeliger received a patent on the machine in 1883, and it was put into immediate use in American shoe factories. In time, machines based on this invention were used in shoe factories throughout the world.

Granville T. Woods. Granville Woods was a talented inventor who was granted one hundred and fifty different patents for inventions in electrical work, steam boilers, and air brakes. He was born in Columbus, Ohio, in 1856 and lived in Cincinnati for part of his life. He started to work in a machine shop and learned a great deal about machinery in this manner. He later worked as a fireman, as an engineer on a railroad, and as an engineer on a steamship line. From his experiences came many of the ideas for his inventions.

Many of the electrical improvements invented by Granville Woods were sold to the American Bell Telephone Company and the General Electric Company. He worked out twelve new devices for electric railways. Other inventions were a steam boiler furnace, an incubator, and an automatic air brake. Perhaps his most dramatic invention was a new kind of telegraph system. This invention made it possible to send telegraph messages to moving trains. Danger warnings sent this way helped reduce train accidents.

The Arts

By the end of the 1800's, talented Negroes had also won recognition for their work in art, literature, and music. During the nineteenth century, Negroes made lasting contributions to American culture.

Painting and Sculpture

Early Negro artists had both talent and a determination to use their talent well. Most had the opportunity to study art at home and abroad. Like many artists, they were given help by sympathetic persons who recognized their talent and wished to see it developed.

Many Negro artists, however, were hampered by a feeling that their work would not be given serious consideration in the United States. They found greater freedom for developing their talent in countries of Europe. In some cases, Negro artists spent most of their adult lives in Europe where they were not restricted by discrimination.

Robert Duncanson.   Robert Duncanson, one of the first successful Negro artists, was born in Cincinnati in 1821. As a teenager, he sketched and painted much of the time. When he reached twenty, his work had attracted the attention of professional artists.

In 1840, the artist received help from the Freedman's Aid Society of Ohio. This organization gave him money to go to Scotland and England for further study. While there, he learned the techniques that brought him fame as a successful landscape artist. One of the landscapes that he painted in England was bought for Windsor Castle.

Many of Robert Duncanson's paintings have been lost. A number of Duncanson paintings were discovered quite by accident. In 1932, an old home was presented to the city of Cincinnati as a museum. Much work went into the restoring of the museum to make it look as it had in the early 1800's. The entrance hall had, over a period of years, been covered with several layers of wallpaper. Workmen carefully removed the wallpaper. Underneath they found a great treasure. Painted on the walls were eight large landscape murals that had been done by Robert Duncanson.

Edmonia Lewis.   In the 1800's, it was unusual for a woman to be an artist. Edmonia Lewis, part-Negro and part-Indian, was born in Boston in 1854. At a very early age, she was placed in an orphanage. She had the good fortune later to be adopted by an abolitionist family. They gave their daughter every advantage, and she attended Oberlin College in Ohio. During her college years, her skill in modeling was noticed. She later went to Boston to receive serious training in sculpture. After some time, she traveled to Italy where she worked and studied in Rome. Most of her adult life was spent in Rome.

Her first successes in sculpture were her portrait busts of famous individuals. Among these were portraits of Abraham Lincoln, John Brown, and Henry Wadsworth Longfellow. Later she completed several groups of full figures in marble that brought her even greater fame. She used both Negro and Indian themes for her work. One of her well-known works was a group called "The Marriage of Hiawatha." Another of her pieces of sculpture, "Forever Free," was of a Negro couple who had just been liberated

"The Blue Hole" by Robert Duncanson

from slavery. Their expressions of both joy and confusion were caught by the artist's skill. Edmonia Lewis had several successful exhibitions of her work. In 1870, there was a Lewis exhibit in Chicago; in 1871, her work was exhibited in Rome; and in 1876, her sculpture was on display in Philadelphia.

Henry Ossawa Tanner.   Henry Tanner was an artist of the same period. His father, a bishop in the African Methodist Church, had hoped the boy would become a minister. Although he never preached a sermon, he expressed a deep and sincere religious feeling through his paintings.

Henry Tanner was born in Pittsburgh in 1859. Even as a young boy, he was fascinated by painting and was determined to study hard to become a good painter. He studied art in Philadelphia and at one time had an exhibition of his paintings in Cincinnati. Interested friends helped Henry Tanner raise money to go to Paris to work and study. While he was there, he completed one of his best-known canvases, "Daniel in the Lion's Den." He continued working in Paris where he was unhampered by racial restrictions.

Henry Tanner then took a trip that had a great influence on his future work. He traveled to Palestine and there received inspiration for other great religious paintings. After this trip, he painted "The Resurrection of Lazarus" and "Christ at the Home of Mary and Martha," and "Annunciation." During his lifetime, Henry Ossawa Tanner received many medals and prizes for his outstanding work. Today his paintings are still treasured. They are in the collections of some of the well-known art museums of the country: the Metropolitan Museum of New York, the Pennsylvania Academy, the Chicago Art Institute, and the Los Angeles Art Gallery.

Literature

Early Negro authors were interested in writing about racial matters. The first authors of the 1800's were runaway slaves who were encouraged by abolitionists to write or dictate the stories of their lives. These early works were used by the abolitionists to prove the evils of slavery. A well-written book of this type was the autobiography of Frederick Douglass entitled *The Life and Times of Frederick Douglass*. The story of this man's progress from slavery to leadership still has interest for the modern reader.

Booker T. Washington was an author as well as an educator. Keenly interested in the welfare of Negroes, he wrote two books about Negro life: *The Future of the American Negro* and *The Negro in Business*. However, the most popular of his books was the story of his own life, *Up from Slavery*. This book showed what achievements were possible for an ambitious and talented person.

The first well-known Negro poet did his writing in the late 1800's. Paul Laurence Dunbar was one generation away from slavery. Both of his parents had been slaves, and neither had had a chance to get an education. Their son did not experience these crushing handicaps. Born in 1872, Paul Laurence Dunbar was free and attended school in Dayton, Ohio. He was the only Negro in his high school class, and he was proud when his classmates chose him as editor of the school paper. Paul Dunbar wrote some poems while he was still in school. His first published poem appeared in a Dayton newspaper when he was just sixteen years old.

After completing high school, Paul Dunbar looked for a job to help support his widowed mother. Although he was ambitious, he had a limited choice of jobs because he was a Negro. The only work he could find was the position of elevator operator in an office building. Young Paul Dunbar kept his books and writing paper by his side in the elevator. When he was not busy, he continued writing poetry.

Determined to see his poems in print, Paul Laurence Dunbar borrowed money to pay for the printing of his first, slim book of poems. Late in 1893, *Oak and Ivy* made its appearance. Paul Dunbar sold copies to his friends and within three weeks was able to pay the publishing bill.

The excellence of his work was immediately recognized after the publication of his second book, *Majors and Minors*. Paul Dun-

Paul Laurence Dunbar

bar's beautiful poetry impressed other poets and writers. James Whitcomb Riley, the Indiana poet, and William Dean Howells of New England gave high praise to the young Ohio poet, who rapidly became famous. His reputation was firmly established when a collection of his first two volumes, *Lyrics of a Lowly Life,* came out in 1896.

In 1897, a great honor was bestowed on Paul Laurence Dunbar. That was the year of the impressive Diamond Jubilee celebration of Queen Victoria's reign as ruler of England. Paul Laurence Dunbar, the Negro poet from Dayton, was invited to read some of his poetry in London during the celebration.

In addition to poetry, Paul Dunbar also wrote short stories. But his poems have found lasting popularity. Many of the poems were written in dialect, reflecting the good-natured humor and the simple lives of the rural Negro. He was only twenty when he wrote one of his best-known poems, "Ode to Ethiopia." Critics who read this poem called Paul Laurence Dunbar the "Poet Laureate of the Negro Race." Part of the poem follows:

> Be proud, my Race, in mind and soul;
> Thy name is writ on Glory's scroll
> In characters of fire.   .
> High 'mid the clouds of Fame's bright sky
> Thy banner's blazoned folds now fly,
> And truth shall lift them higher.

Music

Negroes have made unique contributions to the musical heritage of America. During slavery days, slaves turned to music to express their emotions. Unknown musicians sang about their feelings, and the spirituals and work songs left haunting records of sorrow, of hope for the future, and of comfort in religion. The spirituals have been a decided contribution to American culture.

Another Negro contribution to American culture was the minstrel show, which rose to popularity after the Civil War. James Bland composed many minstrel songs. He was born on Long Island, New York, in 1854. While he was still a young boy, his family moved to Washington, D.C., where his father became the first Negro examiner in the Patent Office. James Bland was a born musician. He made himself a banjo, and, thus equipped, he played and sang songs on the streets of Washington for pennies. When he was fourteen, he was hired as a musician by a hotel keeper. He got more experience by playing for weddings and dinners.

While he was a student at Howard University, he started to write songs. His career was divided between writing music and performing on the stage. He went abroad and lived there for about twenty years, enjoying great popularity both as a composer and as a performer.

James Bland is remembered today for the glorious minstrel songs that he wrote. During his lifetime, he wrote close to seven hundred songs. One of the best-loved is "In the Evening by the Moonlight." In 1940, the state of Virginia adopted James Bland's "Carry Me Back to Old Virginny" as its official state song.

Medicine

Medical history was made in the year 1893. The place was at Provident Hospital in Chicago. The patient was James Cornish, a man who had received a knife wound in an artery close to his heart. His chances for survival were slim, for doctors knew little about heart injuries at that time. The doctor was Dr. Daniel Hale Williams, who decided upon a daring new treatment to save his patient's life. He would operate and sew up the wound. With six assistants, Dr. Williams performed the first successful heart operation on record; and the patient lived. A Chicago newspaper carried the headline, "Sewed Up His Heart!"

Daniel Hale Williams had done other remarkable things in his lifetime. He valued the friendship of both white and Negro citizens who gave help for some of his projects. His first ambitions to become a doctor were encouraged by a white doctor who lived in Illinois. The help of several friends made it possible for him to study medicine at the Chicago Medical College. Upon graduation, young Dr. Williams opened an office, but there was no hospital which permitted Negro doctors to operate. Dr. Williams did something about this. He again depended upon the help of many persons, both Negro and white, to help him establish Provident Hospital in Chicago. In this hospital, any doctor could operate regardless of his race. In connection with this hospital, Dr. Williams started the first training center for Negro nurses in the country. He himself was on the staff of the hospital, and his skill as a surgeon won the respect of the medical profession. Three years later in 1893, he was called to Washington, D.C., to take charge of the Freedmen's Hospital there. During the five years he was there, many improvements were made.

Dr. Williams returned to Chicago in 1898 and continued using his skill to help those in need. He also spent much of his time in traveling and giving lectures, particularly in the South. He worked with other interested citizens to help establish hospitals and medical training centers for Negroes in other American cities.

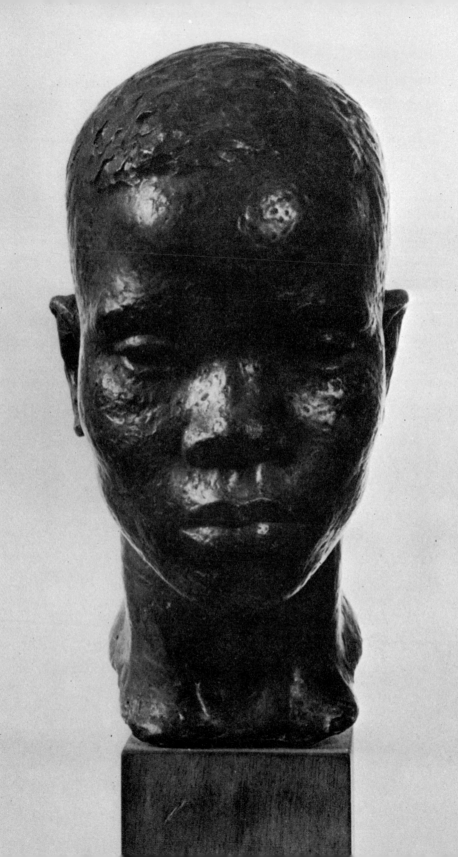

Early Twentieth Century:
1900—1929

By the beginning of the new century, the United States had become an industrial giant. Scientific knowledge had been put to work, and everyday uses of steam and electricity had brought changes in the lives of people. These sources of power had improved methods of transportation and communication. They had completely revolutionized manufacturing and had caused our nation to become a leader in the production of manufactured goods. Progress in industry had caused a rapid growth of large cities. People who remembered the good old days back on the farm had to adjust to changes in their way of living.

Changes were coming to Negro life, too. In 1900, about three quarters of all American Negroes were still living in rural areas in the South though some had moved to cities, especially northern cities, to find better jobs. See Appendix II, at the back of the book, for more detailed figures. They found problems in the

"Shoeshine Boy" by Richmond Barthé

North, too. Housing was limited to certain segregated sections of the cities. So many Negroes moving into the cities caused over-crowding in their districts, and Negroes were prohibited from finding homes in white sections. Houses in Negro sections were often old and badly in need of repair. Unsatisfactory sanitary con-ditions contributed to a high degree of disease and poor health.

In spite of these oppressive handicaps, some Negroes did suc-ceed in finding the better life they were seeking. Some skilled and talented individuals were able to make a more comfortable liv-ing. In cities, education was easier for Negroes to obtain. More young men and women attended college, and their training pre-pared them to take a more active part in the progress of the na-tion. Among the well-educated Negroes were individuals who were deeply concerned about the welfare of their race. Many of them worked to improve conditions and opportunities for Ne-groes.

In the first years of the twentieth century, there were three important developments that affected Negro life in our country. First, Negroes themselves took an active part in establishing or-ganizations for Negro advancement. Second, World War I had a tremendous impact upon the lives of thousands of Negro citi-zens. A third important development was the outstanding achieve-ment made by Negroes in art, music, literature, entertainment, sports, business, and education.

Organizations for Negro Advancement

In 1900, Booker T. Washington was the recognized leader of Negro affairs in the United States. Although admired by the majority of Negroes, his leadership was not accepted by all Ne-groes. Well-educated Negroes were becoming dissatisfied with some of Washington's theories. They especially objected to his idea that social and political progress for the Negro were less im-portant than finding satisfactory jobs. Although they agreed that vocational training was necessary, they also felt strongly that an academic college education should be open to talented individuals who would become leaders of the race. They opposed all forms of racial discrimination that prevented Negroes from enjoying the full privileges of citizenship.

The Niagara Movement

A group of young Negro intellectuals met at Niagara Falls, Canada, in 1905 to work out solutions to racial problems. The leader of the group was William Edward Burghardt Du Bois, an

W. E. B. Du Bois

educator and author. Du Bois openly criticized Booker T. Washington's idea of solving the Negro's problems through a first step of job training. Born in Great Barrington, Massachusetts, of free parents, W. E. B. Du Bois had had the advantage of an excellent education. He was graduated from Fisk University in Nashville and then received a Master's degree from Harvard University. After continuing his studies at the University of Berlin in Germany, he returned to Harvard where he received a Doctor of

Philosophy degree. He was the first Negro to receive a Ph.D. from Harvard. In his book, *The Souls of Black Folk,* he presented a study of problems faced by the American Negro and remarked that the big problem of the twentieth century would be the problem of "the color line." Not content merely to study problems, he was determined to act.

Du Bois organized the Niagara Movement. Its purpose was to try to bring an end to racial discrimination. Members would work with individuals of all races to bring about improvements. The Niagara Movement was never a strong organization that appealed to great numbers of people, but it was always an important one. It proved that Negro leaders had analyzed the problem of their situation and were ready to work together. After 1908, the leaders of the Niagara Movement were invited to join with whites in a new organization, the National Association for the Advancement of Colored People. Attention turned to this new group.

The National Association for the
Advancement of Colored People

It was clear in the early 1900's that Negroes faced real problems because of racial discrimination. Jim Crow laws were in effect in all sections of the country. Many jobs were closed to Negroes, and Negro workers were often paid lower salaries for the work they did. There were some cases where distrust and ill-feeling between the races exploded into violence. Thinking citizens of both races were concerned about these conditions. In 1909, a group of interested white and Negro individuals met in New York to discuss the problem.

One of the leaders of the group was Mary White Ovington, a white social worker. As a reporter who gathered news about the Niagara Movement, she had become interested in the efforts of people working together. She felt that a strong organization would need white as well as Negro members. She invited W. E. B. Du Bois and other members of the Niagara Movement to attend the conference in New York. Another important leader was Henry Moskowitz, a Jewish social worker. From this New York meeting, the National Association for the Advancement of Colored People was formed. From its beginning, the NAACP has worked to protect the citizenship rights of Negroes. The organization has opposed all forms of racial segregation and discrimination.

Leaders of the NAACP decided to work for the Negro cause in two ways, through legal action and through publicity and public education. W. E. B. Du Bois founded and edited the organization's publication, *The Crisis*. This magazine gave publicity to the

Cover of The Crisis *showing a Negro dressed as a warrior.*

work of the NAACP. It printed stories of Negro achievement and contained works of Negro artists. Du Bois admired the Communist Revolution and the new Union of Soviet Socialist Republics. Arguing that more of an activist stand be taken, he broke with the NAACP in the mid 1930's, and eventually went to Ghana, where he became an active citizen. He joined the Communist party in 1961 at the age of 93 and died in 1963.

The NAACP defended Negroes' rights in court. It was active in working for the right to vote. It brought legal action against the grandfather clauses until 1915, when the Supreme Court of the United States ruled grandfather clauses unconstitutional. The organization challenged Jim Crow laws and worked for equal pay for Negro workers. As its work brought actual improvements, the NAACP became stronger and opened active branches in cities other than New York. The first branch office was established in Chicago. By 1918, there were eighty branches of the association. One year later there were three hundred branches. As it gained in strength and membership, the association continued to recruit both Negro and white members. Today it is a powerful bi-racial organization which works constantly for the civil rights of Negroes.

The National Urban League

Thousands of Negroes who left the South to seek better jobs in large northern cities had been used to living on farms and were confused by the change to city life. Finding a job was often difficult, for the newcomers lacked experience and training. In some cases, even finding a place to live was a problem. These people needed help until they could learn to take care of themselves in new surroundings.

Due largely to the foresight of George Edmond Haynes, an organization was founded to help Negroes in cities. A Negro sociologist, Dr. Haynes received his Ph.D. from Columbia University. During his graduate studies, he had analyzed population

Negroes moved to Harlem and other cities of the North.

migrations. He found that large numbers of Negroes were migrating to industrial centers. Realizing the change from rural to city living would be difficult, Dr. Haynes foresaw the need for trained social workers to help newcomers learn to live in cities.

On May 19, 1910, the National Urban League was formed. It was first called the Committee on Urban Conditions Among Negroes in New York, but the name was later shortened. Dr. Haynes served as the first Executive Director of the organization, an office he held until 1918.

Like the NAACP, the National Urban League is composed of white and Negro members. Mrs. William Baldwin, Jr., one of the co-founders, summed up the major goal of the National Urban League. "Let us work not as colored people, nor as white people, for the narrow good of any group alone; but rather as American citizens for the common good of our common city, our common country."

The League helped find jobs and homes. Newcomers to the city were interviewed about their training and skills and then were told about suitable jobs. The League also helped Negroes become members of labor unions. Information was given about housing. Persons with particular problems were sent to a social service agency for help. In some cities, the League organized groups of Big Brothers and Big Sisters to work with children who needed guidance. Visiting teachers were sometimes provided. The League printed its own magazine called *Opportunity*, which contained the writings of Negro authors and poets. In many ways, the work of the National Urban League smoothed the way of Negroes who migrated to the North.

This organization has always had outstanding leadership. Eugene Kinckle Jones served as Executive Secretary from 1911 to 1941. When asked what the League hoped to accomplish eventually, Mr. Jones answered, "To work itself out of a job." Then he went on to explain that when equal opportunities were extended to members of all races, the work of the League would be over.

In 1941, Lester Blackwell Granger became Executive Director of the National Urban League. Well-trained in social work, Lester

Granger continued to work for greater equality of opportunity. During World War II, he served as a special advisor to the Secretary of the Navy, James Forrestal. His recommendations for the integration of Navy servicemen played a major part in the eventual desegregation of the Navy.

Since 1961, Whitney M. Young, Jr., has headed the organization. Under his leadership, the National Urban League has endorsed special aid to Negro education, widespread opportunities for Negroes in business, elimination of racial ghettos, and greater health and welfare services. In short, the National Urban League is still trying to work itself out of a job by reaching the goal of equal opportunities for all.

World War I

A crisis in Europe brought many changes into the lives of all American citizens. In August 1914, the continent of Europe was plunged into war. About three years later, the United States was drawn into the war effort. Negro and white soldiers were called upon to defend their country and fight against a common enemy. White and Negro workers alike were called upon to produce the supplies that were necessary for a country at war. During these years, the loyalty and patriotism of all citizens were required to give strength and unity to our country. Among the armed forces, there were heroes from both races. Their courageous actions proved that they were American citizens first, rather than Negro or white citizens.

The Great Migration

After the war in Europe started, thousands of Negroes moved northward. There were several reasons for this mass migration, as it was called. The main hope of those who moved now, was the same as of those few who had moved earlier; it was still the promise of better living and working conditions and better schools. Negro newspapers had developed in many northern cities. One

AN EDITORIAL ON

THE N. A. A. C. P.

FROM

JAN. 6, 1923

UNJUST CRITICISM

IN VIEW of criticism passed upon the National Association for the Advancement of Colored People emanating from certain sources and selfish individuals, it is timely to point out some of the aims, objects and purposes of this splendid and magnificent organization. It is a well known fact that many years ago propaganda was cunningly organized and put on foot the purpose of which was to poison the public mind against Colored Americans, which has resulted in the curtailment and in some localities a complete denial of the civil and political rights of our Race.

THIS SPIRIT has developed to such an extent as to make its baneful influence felt and in a large measure recognized by the two major political parties. A number of friends and supporters of the civil and political rights of our group, both white and Colored, seeing the evil effects of this propaganda, conceived the idea of bringing into existence an effective organization to combat the same; hence this association. It has done a wonderful work during its few years of existence. It not only has representatives at the capital of every state when the legislature is in session, but also at Washington when Congress is in session.

IT COMBATS every move that is made and every step that is taken inimical to the Colored Race. It was chiefly through this organization that residential segregation was declared unconstitutional by the United States Supreme Court. It was also due largely to the fight made by this organization that the Dyer anti-lynching bill passed the House, and although temporarily defeated in the Senate, if such a measure should ultimately become a law, as we believe it will, it will be due chiefly to the work of this organization.

NOT ONLY Colored Americans but every white friend of liberty, justice, fair play and a square deal should belong to this organization. It is strictly nonpartisan. It sustains the same relation to the Colored Race that the anti-saloon league sustains to the cause of prohibition and that the American Federation of Labor sustains to the cause of labor. The anti-saloon league supports candidates who are in favor of prohibition and opposes those who are against prohibition, regardless of their party affiliations. The American Federation of Labor supports those who are favorable to their cause and opposes those who are against it, regardless of their party affiliations. The N. A. A. C. P. likewise supports the candidates who are favorable to the cause they deem vital and paramount and opposes those who are against it, regardless of their party affiliations.

—Reprinted by the National Association for the Advancement of Colored People, 70 Fifth Aveaue, New York City.

This editorial urges support of the NAACP.

example was *The Chicago Defender,* edited by the talented writer Robert Abbott. This newspaper carried news of Negro life and had a wide circulation in every part of the country. *The Chicago Defender* had news stories about opportunities in northern cities: higher wages, better schools for children, the right to vote, and better recreational facilities. News written in this and other newspapers influenced many people to move north.

There was a real need for more workers in large industrial plants. For years, most of the skilled workers had been immigrants from Europe. Because of the war in Europe, few immigrants came to America after 1914. There were fewer workers to fill the jobs that were available. In addition, industry was growing, and many more workers were needed. To ease the shortage of labor, special labor agents traveled to the South to recruit workers. Their descriptions of plentiful jobs and high wages caused even more families to move northward. During the migration years, from 1914 to 1920, a half million to a million Negroes flocked into the industrial centers of the North. Although there were difficulties in adjusting to new surroundings, many people found the better jobs and schools that they were seeking.

Negroes in World War I

The United States entered the war on April 6, 1917. As in the past, Negro volunteers joined other Americans to serve in the armed forces. During the war years, one-half million Negroes wore the military uniforms of the United States, and many of these men served brilliantly. One example of high courage was the record of the 369th Infantry, a company made up entirely of Negro soldiers. The 369th was cited for bravery on eleven different occasions. This entire company was awarded the highest military honor of the French Army, the Croix de Guerre, for its "gallantry in action" while fighting in France.

Two soldiers of this company represent the kind of courage that made the 369th a top fighting unit. They were Sergeant Henry Johnson of Albany, New York, and Needham Roberts of Trenton, New Jersey. The two men were on guard duty at a remote outpost on May 14, 1918. At dawn, they were attacked by about twenty German soldiers. Though wounded and outnumbered, the two American soldiers fought back until their ammunition was gone. At that point, a German soldier started to drag Roberts away as a prisoner-of-war. Sergeant Henry Johnson grabbed the only weapons at hand. He had a knife and his rifle, without bullets, became a club. Using these, Sergeant Johnson fought off the German soldier and freed Roberts. Together the two men fought so fiercely that they wounded several of the Germans. The others retreated. Johnson and Roberts returned to the American lines under their own power. For this display of courage, each received an individual Croix de Guerre. Moreover, in a letter to Johnson's wife, Colonel Hayward wrote, "The Germans, doubtless thinking it was a host instead of two brave colored boys fighting like tigers at bay, picked up their dead and wounded and slunk away, leaving many weapons and a part of their shot-riddled clothing and leaving a trail of blood, which we followed at dawn near to their lines." [1]

Another hero was Sergeant Rufus B. Atwood, who repaired communication lines under fire. On November 10, 1918, a house which contained the switchboard of an important communications center was struck by a shell. Working under constant shelling, Sergeant Atwood repaired the switchboard and connected the damaged lines. His work was useless, however, for an ammunition dump nearby was soon struck and it exploded only to wreck the switchboard once more. Disregarding personal danger, Sergeant Atwood rebuilt the switchboard a second time and carefully made new electrical connections. Because of his courage, the important communications center remained in operation.

There were other instances of individual and group heroism. The American soldier was a fighting man who won the respect of his country. Negroes were an important part of American military units. General John Pershing, the commander of the American forces in Europe, had this to say about their performance, "I

[1] John Hope Franklin, *From Slavery to Freedom* (New York: Alfred A. Knopf, Inc., 1956), p. 458.

Segregated troops arrive in France during World War I.

cannot commend too highly the spirit shown among the colored combat troops, who exhibit fine capacity for quick training and eagerness for the most dangerous service." [2]

[2] Merl Eppse, *The Negro Too in American History* (Nashville: The National Publishing Company, 1943), p. 312.

After the War

When World War I came to a close, the American people were eager to forget about the war years. They were anxious to return to normal living. Thousands of soldiers returned home, prepared to pick up once more the familiar way of living during peace. Negroes, however, did not want to return to the days before the war. They had held good jobs during the war when there had been a shortage of workers. After the war, competition for jobs was keen, and Negroes were unwilling to be pushed back into types of work with lower pay.

Once more bitter feelings between the races developed in some parts of the country. The Ku Klux Klan was revived, and branches of this group were active even in northern states. Lawless action against Negroes grew more frequent. In 1919, a wave of race riots erupted in various cities in the North and South. The hysterical actions of mobs resulted in the burning of homes and property. Individuals were attacked, and there were numerous instances of floggings, lynchings, and murders. Hundreds of persons of both races were wounded and many killed during this period of racial tension.

In face of the hysteria and violence, the NAACP set up a program to fight against racial injustice. This organization started a crusade against lynching and thoroughly investigated such crimes. Publicity given to the causes and tragic results of mob violence helped influence public opinion. Although there were fewer instances of racial outbreaks, they did not disappear completely from the American scene.

One by now familiar answer to racial discrimination was offered by Marcus Garvey, who believed that Negroes could never be successful in the United States. Proud of his race, Garvey started a campaign of "Back to Africa" for all Africans. Marcus Garvey was familiar with Negro problems in several sections of the world. He was born in Jamaica in 1887. As an adult in Jamaica, he could not find work as a printer because of his color. He went to England where he found work in a publishing company. While in England, his idea of Africa for Africans began to take form. He returned to Jamaica in 1914 and founded the Universal Negro Improvement Association. The aim of this organization was to start a colony in Africa for all the Negroes of the world.

Marcus Garvey

Marcus Garvey came to the United States in 1916. He started an American branch of the Universal Negro Improvement Association and continued working for the Back-to-Africa movement. He attracted members to his organization by appealing to racial pride. Praising everything black, he stated that blackness stood for strength and beauty. He staged colorful parades in which members wore elaborate uniforms. Thousands of Negroes joined the organization. Marcus Garvey was convicted on charges of using the mail to defraud in connection with a business venture, The Black Star Steamship Line, in 1925. He was sent back to Jamaica in 1927.

Many historians feel that the popularity of the Garvey movement was based on the fact that it encouraged Negroes to express a pride in their race. Few of the followers of Garvey had any real intention of moving to Africa. Negroes had had a long history of helping to build America, and most had no wish to leave their native land. They hoped to stay here and get rid of racial discrimination in their own country.

A Sidelight: Exploration to the North Pole

The adventurous life of an explorer was hard to come by in the 1900's, for there were few unknown lands left to explore. The frozen territory close to the North and South Poles appealed to adventurers. The famous Polar explorer, Admiral Robert Peary, started his exploration of the North Pole area in the 1890's. Matthew Henson, a Negro adventurer, went with Peary. At first he was Peary's servant, but gradually, because of his great ability and usefulness, he became a valuable assistant with important responsibilities. He was expert in handling Eskimo husky dogs, the only transportation in the frozen wilderness. Matthew Henson also had an unusual talent for making friends with the Eskimo people, even learning some of their language. The resulting friendship and cooperation of the Eskimos were helpful to the exploring party.

Peary's ambition to locate the North Pole was not successful in 1897. Three other unsuccessful explorations were carried out in 1900, 1902, and 1905. Through these years of discouragement, Matthew Henson shared Admiral Peary's hardships and disappointments. In 1908, another expedition to reach the North Pole was formed. Both Henson and Peary felt that this was their last chance; they had to be successful or give up their ambition.

Matthew Henson, right, with three North Pole explorers.

They were willing to suffer the extreme hardships once more: frostbite, blizzards, snow blindness, and frigid temperatures. On April 4, 1909, an advance group made up of Peary, Henson, and four Eskimos was still sixty miles from the destination. It took three long days by dogsled to reach the exact location. After checking his careful calculations once more, Admiral Peary handed the American flag to his friend and assistant, Matthew Henson. It was Henson who had the honor of placing the flag on the North Pole on April 6, 1909. This act proved that the outpost had been discovered by explorers from the United States.

On the forty-fifth anniversary of this important discovery, Matthew Henson, the Negro explorer, was invited to the White House by President Eisenhower. Once more he received recognition and honor for his part in the successful exploration.

The Arts and Education

In the early 1900's, more Negroes than at any time had the advantage of a better education and improved living conditions. With their newly developing pride in their own race and the self-confidence that came with pride, they were determined to have a larger share of the benefits of American life. Artists expressed their feelings, often about racial conflict, through writing, art, or music. W. E. B. Du Bois, one of the early outstanding authors of the twentieth century, wrote such books as *Black Reconstruction* and *The Souls of Black Folk*. Magazines like *Opportunity* emphasized Negro progress and encouraged feelings of Negro worth. Newspapers like the *The Chicago Defender* supplied information about Negro life and happenings. Operating at a time when most city newspapers ignored the Negro as news, the Negro newspapers were the only source of this kind of information. These newspapers were sold in all sections of the country, and the subscribers were Negroes who wanted to keep informed about their race. In recent years, the influence of all-Negro newspapers has lessened; Negroes are no longer excluded from regular news channels.

In the 1920's, many Negroes were working successfully in art, literature, and music. The 1920's were sometimes called the Negro Renaissance because of the interest and participation in the arts. The achievement of Negroes in the arts carried over into other areas of American life. Talented Negroes in every occupation had finally received enough training to compete with white individuals with similar talents. Successful persons gained fame, not because they were Negroes but because their accomplishments had value.

Literature

James Weldon Johnson.   Starting his writing career before the Renaissance period of the twenties, James Weldon Johnson was a man of many talents. In his lifetime, he was an educator, a lawyer, an official in the NAACP, and a diplomat to foreign countries, as well as an author. One of his novels was *The Autobiography of an Ex-Coloured Man,* published in 1912. In 1900, he wrote his best-known poem, "Lift Every Voice and Sing." This poem was set to music by his talented brother, J. Rosamond Johnson. In time, it became a sort of national song which expressed the deep faith in freedom held by many American Negroes. Part of the poem reads:

> Lift ev'ry voice and sing
> Till earth and heaven ring.
> Ring with the harmonies of Liberty;
> Let our rejoicing rise
> High as the list'ning skies,
> Let it resound loud as the rolling sea.
> Sing a song full of faith that the dark past has taught us,
> Sing a song full of hope that the present has brought us.
> Facing the rising sun of our new day begun,
> Let us march on till victory is won.

James Weldon Johnson continued writing through the 1920's and 1930's. In 1922, he published *The Book of American Negro Poetry* in which he showed the contributions that Negro poets had made. His dramatic poem "God's Trombones" appeared in 1927; it was a series of "Seven Sermons in Verse" and included "The Creation." In 1933, his autobiography, *Along This Way,* was printed.

Countee Cullen. One of the leading poets of the period was Countee Cullen. His first book of poetry, *Color,* was published when he was only twenty-one years old. He had an excellent education which helped him develop his talent to a high degree. While a student at New York University, he won the Witter Bynner poetry prize for college students. He graduated with honors, earning a Phi Beta Kappa key. He then went to Harvard for an M.A. degree. Countee Cullen wrote several other volumes of poetry, including *The Ballad of the Brown Girl* and *Copper Sun.* The one novel he wrote is entitled *One Way to Heaven.*

Langston Hughes.   A writer of great versatility, Langston Hughes has published poetry, novels, histories, biographies, plays, and even songs. Like Countee Cullen, he won the Witter Bynner poetry prize while studying at Columbia University. His writings have brought him other awards and honors, as well. Langston Hughes is known mainly for books of verse such as *The Dream Keeper, Shakespeare in Harlem,* and *One Way Ticket.*

There were many other noteworthy authors of the period. Some historians feel that Claude McKay's bitter poetry in *Harlem Shadows* was the beginning of the whole Renaissance period. Arna Bontemps, Walter White, Jean Toomer, and Jessie Fauset made significant contributions. Alain Locke, one of the leaders of the literary movement, wrote an important book called *The New Negro* in 1925. An educator as well as an author, Alain Locke analyzed the work that was being done by Negro writers. He stated that the Negro author had come of age. He also thought that the work of Negro authors should be judged in competition with the works of all writers. Alain Locke expressed a belief that through the arts all races could be drawn closer together in understanding.

Painting and Sculpture

Art as a form of expression during the Negro Renaissance developed later than literature. Among the early artists were the following two.

Aaron Douglas.   A painter of scenes of Negro life, Aaron Douglas studied in both Philadelphia and Paris. He designed illustrations and jackets for the books of prominent Negroes. Books by Countee Cullen, Langston Hughes, and James Weldon Johnson contained original illustrations by Douglas. Some of his larger works of art are murals painted for the Harlem branch of the Y.M.C.A. and a branch of the New York Public Library. A Douglas mural hangs in the library of Fisk University, where he had taught and headed the fine arts department.

Richmond Barthé. A talented sculptor, Richmond Barthé was first interested in painting, which he studied at the Art Institute in Chicago. Even as a student, he was skillful in painting portraits. He was starting a successful career as a portrait painter when one of his teachers recognized an unusual talent in sculpturing. He persuaded the young artist to concentrate on this form of art work. His judgment was correct, for today Richmond Barthé is considered one of the finest American sculptors. Among his best-known works are "Shoeshine Boy," "The Harmonica Player," and "Boxer." Barthé's work is so distinguished that examples of his sculpture are exhibited in some of the leading art museums of the nation: the Metropolitan Museum of Art in New York, the Pennsylvania Academy of Fine Arts, the Philadelphia Museum, and the Art Institute of Chicago, where he received his training. In addition, his works are displayed in museums in England, Germany, France, and Africa.

Notable artists from the later period, the 1930's and 1940's, included Laura Waring, Charles Alston, Sargent Johnson, Archibald Motley, and Hughie Lee-Smith.

Composers, Directors, and Singers

During the Negro Renaissance, performers of serious music reached great heights. This is a difficult field in which to excel since even the greatest musical talent requires long years of expensive study and training. The lives of successful musical artists show their struggles and determination in preparing for their careers.

Nathaniel Dett spent years of study in the finest music schools before undertaking his work of composing music. Today, his "Listen to the Lambs" and "Oh, Holy Lord" are favorites of many choral groups; and the "Juba Dance" is equally well known. He later composed an opera, "The Ordering of Moses," which was first performed in the 1940's. Paul Robeson's powerful baritone

On pages 174 and 175:
"Boy with Tyre" by Hughie Lee-Smith

voice brought him great success as a concert singer both in the United States and abroad. The grandson of a slave, Robeson was graduated from Rutgers University and attended Columbia Law School before he turned his attention to acting in 1924. He is known for his interpretation of the title role in Eugene O'Neill's *Emperor Jones,* his singing of "Ol' Man River" in *Showboat,* both during the 1920's, and his interpretations of Negro spirituals. In London during the 1930's and in New York during the 1940's, he was cited for his outstanding performance as Othello. After these triumphs, Robeson was mentioned less frequently in news accounts, and his name became linked with Communist causes.

During the 1930's, Dean Dixon was training to become a conductor of a symphony orchestra. He proved his talents by guest-conducting some of the largest American orchestras, the New York Philharmonic Symphony, the NBC Summer Symphony, and the National Youth Administration Orchestra. His talent and excellent training were not strong enough to overcome prejudice, and Dean Dixon could not find a permanent appointment in the United States. When he went to Europe where racial discrimination was not a barrier, his talent was recognized. He became the regular conductor of symphony orchestras in Germany, Italy, Sweden, and Australia.

Harry Burleigh.   A successful composer and singer, Harry Burleigh had always loved music. As a small boy, he would stand outside the windows of the house where his mother worked as a maid just to hear the piano music drifting out. When he grew older, he developed his voice by singing in choirs and studying music. His voice was excellent. When he heard that a fashionable New York church was having try-outs for a baritone solo voice, Harry Burleigh entered the competition. He got the job and became the only Negro singer in the all-white church.

Harry Burleigh had a particular fondness for the spirituals handed down through so many generations. He composed musical arrangements for many of them so that they could be sung in concert halls. Among the many Burleigh arrangements are "Ain't

Goin' to Study War No Mo'," "Deep River," "Ev-ry Time I Feel the Spirit," and "Sometimes I Feel Like a Motherless Child."

Roland Hayes. One of America's great tenors was Roland Hayes. Born in Georgia in 1887, Roland loved music. His father encouraged him to sing. His talent was noticed when he was very young, for he seemed to sing as easily as he breathed.

A series of recordings helped Roland Hayes decide what he wanted to be. When he heard records made by the great Italian tenor Enrico Caruso, he was so impressed that he decided to become a professional singer. He went to Fisk University and became a member of the Jubilee Singers. He was part of that group when it made its first singing tour of the North. One of the concerts was held in Boston, and Roland Hayes remained there to begin serious work in voice training. Working at odd jobs to pay for his lessons, he gained experience and confidence by singing in Negro churches and schools. By 1916, he felt that his voice was ready for a concert tour.

Unknown singers often experience difficulties in attracting audiences at the beginning of their careers. Roland Hayes had even greater difficulties than most young artists, for American audiences were not accustomed to Negro singers on the concert stage. Roland Hayes scheduled a series of tours, mainly for Negro organizations: churches, schools, and colleges. He arranged for a concert at Boston Symphony Hall. The critical reviews of this concert were excellent. They gave the young musician the encouragement to try to seek recognition of his talent in Europe.

Roland Hayes' concert tour of Europe was a marked success. In England, he gave a command performance in Buckingham Palace before King George V. This was the turning point in his career. From that point forward, he was in great demand as a concert singer in European countries. After his reputation had been established abroad, he enjoyed great success in the United States. Even during his most successful years, Roland Hayes insisted that some of the seats to his concerts be sold at a low cost. He wanted to make sure that poorer people of all races could attend if they wished. A pioneer in the field of classical music, Roland Hayes was the first concert singer of his race to reach lasting fame.

Marian Anderson. "She has a voice that is heard only once in a hundred years." So said the famous musician Arturo Toscanini, when he heard Marian Anderson sing. It was a thrilling day and a wonderful concert for Marian Anderson; perhaps she remembered her struggles of many years to reach that day.

She was born in Philadelphia in 1908. Her early life was unusually happy, for the Anderson family was close-knit. Both Marian and her two younger sisters loved to sing, and all three sang in the children's choir in the church. Marian's voice was so beautiful that she became a regular member of the adult choir when she was just thirteen years old. She frequently sang solo parts and would substitute for absent soloists. It didn't matter whether the part was bass, tenor, alto, or soprano. Marian could sing them all! While she was a student in high school, she was giving short concerts in a number of churches. At one of these concerts, Roland Hayes heard her sing. He talked to Marian and her mother and urged them to start music lessons for the talented girl.

Preparing for a career in music presented immediate problems. Scarcity of money was one, but Marian Anderson's talent was so obvious that many persons gave help. Her first teacher recognized the girl's unusual gift and taught her without charge. Marian's church helped to supply money for other training. A special concert, which featured Roland Hayes as a soloist, was held at the church, and the money collected was given to Marian for voice lessons. She spent many years studying and gaining experience by singing in churches and schools.

Another problem that Marian Anderson faced was that of discrimination. She never forgot the unpleasant experience she had when she tried to enroll in a music school in Philadelphia. Young, unsure of herself, she waited in line to ask for information. When her turn came, she was ignored. Finally everyone in the line be-

Marian Anderson

hind her had been interviewed, and Marian was the only one left waiting. Then, she was curtly informed, "We don't take colored!"

Traveling into different sections of the country was also difficult. Even as a young singer, Marian Anderson hated to ride in the inferior and usually dirty Jim Crow railroad cars. When she became more successful, traveling continued to present problems. In the South, she often spent the night in private homes because there were few comfortable hotel accommodations for Negroes. In spite of these and other difficulties, Marian Anderson continued training for her career.

In 1927 she entered a contest in which three hundred singers were competing for the chance to be a guest soloist with the New York Philharmonic Orchestra. Marian Anderson was the winner. After this experience, she began making appearances as a concert singer. Although she was modestly successful, Marian Anderson was not satisfied with the progress of her career. She wanted to appear in all the big cities.

Feeling that she was at a standstill, she went to Europe in the mid-1930's for more study and a tour of concerts. Here she felt that her color was not the obstacle it had been in the United States. People seemed to accept her, and she felt comfortable. Her first large concert was in Berlin, Germany. A later tour of the Scandinavian countries was heart-warming, for there her singing was received with great enthusiasm. Wherever she sang in Europe, she won the acclaim of audiences and critics. As a result of her triumphs in Europe, Marian Anderson returned to the United States with the reputation of a highly successful concert star.

After her reputation had been established, her talents were highly praised in her own country. She was asked to sing in many cities, and her concerts were usually sell-outs. But even at the height of her career she felt the force of discrimination. One well-known instance took place in Washington, D.C. Arrangements were made for her to give a concert in Constitution Hall. The owners of the hall, the Daughters of the American Revolution, refused to allow her to make an appearance there only because she was a Negro. The concert was canceled amid a furor of publicity. People throughout the nation were indignant. Newspapers carried the story in bold headlines, and other musicians refused to appear in Constitution Hall.

Marian Anderson did give a concert in Washington; she received a special invitation to sing, with the Lincoln Memorial as a stage. On Easter Sunday, 1939, Marian Anderson faced a Washington audience of thousands of people. They crowded the Mall in front of the Lincoln Memorial as far as her eyes could see. Throughout the concert, they showed enthusiasm for the songs and their approval of the truly great talent of the singer.

In time, the owners of Constitution Hall lifted the ban against Negro artists. Marian Anderson eventually sang there several times. Because of her outstanding talent, she was able to overcome another barrier of discrimination. She was the first Negro singer to become a member of the Metropolitan Opera Company. When she was chosen to make her debut in 1955, she was thrilled by the personal triumph. At the same time, she was thinking of those who might follow in her footsteps. She expressed her feelings by saying, "The chance to be a member of the Metropolitan has been a highlight of my life. It has meant much to me and to my people. If I have been privileged to serve as a symbol, to be the first Negro to sing as a regular member of the Company, I take greater pride from knowing that it has encouraged other singers of my group to realize that doors everywhere may open increasingly to those who have prepared themselves well." [3] In 1958 she was appointed an alternate delegate at the United Nations.

Jazz and Entertainment

During the 1920's, jazz, an invention of the American Negro and one of the most vital contributions of America to the world of music, caught fire and became popular across the country. Indeed, the Roaring Twenties were also referred to as the Jazz Age.

[3] Marian Anderson, *My Lord, What a Morning* (New York: Viking Press, 1963), p. 304.

Piano syncopation was known in the United States in the 1890's, and during World War I white bands in Chicago were imitating the sound of jazz. Jazz and the blues provided the popular tunes of the day, and the vaudeville stage produced new stars who danced, sang, or played comedy roles.

W. C. Handy.   "The Father of the Blues" was William Christopher Handy, who led a roving life through the cities of the South. Working at odd jobs, he sometimes had so little money that he had to sleep out in the open. Those were the hard times he remembered when he wrote the famous line, "I hate to see the evening sun go down." Wherever he worked, W. C. Handy listened to the songs and chants of other working people. He heard expressions of longing and sadness, despair and hope. These were the feelings that he wrote into his songs. His first song was "Memphis Blues." Later he wrote "Beale Street Blues" and then the always popular "St. Louis Blues." Many other compositions followed, and the haunting melodies of W. C. Handy have become a very real part of America's musical background. Today a statue of Handy, trumpet in hand, is located in Handy Park in Memphis, Tennessee.

Louis Armstrong.   Another man with a trumpet has played in so many countries of the world that he has been nicknamed the "Ambassador of Jazz." Louis "Satchmo" Armstrong began life under unfavorable conditions. Born in the slums of New Orleans, he was well acquainted with hunger and neglect. He was sent to a Waif's Home for Boys when he was thirteen, and there he received the encouragement he needed to develop his interest in music. Largely self-taught, Louis Armstrong worked out his own unique style of playing jazz on the trumpet. When he played with bands throughout the country, his popularity grew. In 1926, a New York theater advertised his appearance with a lighted sign that read, "The World's Greatest Trumpeter." His skill with the trumpet led him to many places: to packed theaters in European countries, to a command performance before King George VI of England, to enthusiastic Russians who understood the universal appeal of jazz.

Bert Williams. Vaudeville gave Bert Williams a chance to develop his side-splitting comedy routine. Rather a serious man in real life, Bert Williams on stage played the part of a lazy, bumbling character whose ridiculous antics left the audience weak with laughter. Success in New York was followed by a profitable tour of England. Bert Williams later joined the famous Ziegfeld Follies and went on to new triumphs.

Bill Robinson. Another famous entertainer won fame because of his nimble feet. Bill "Bojangles" Robinson made complicated dance steps look easier than walking and a lot more fun. He never took a dancing lesson in his life, and few dancers have matched his skill. His dancing feet made him a rich man as he starred in vaudeville, in musical comedies, and in the movies. He seemed to thrive on the strenuous life of a dancer. When he was sixty-one years old, he danced down sixty-one blocks of Broadway to celebrate the event.

Duke Ellington, the composer and band leader, wrote such lasting melodies as "Mood Indigo" and "Sophisticated Lady." The Mills Brothers popularized the smooth harmonies of quartet singing. Ethel Waters starred in musical comedies on the stage and in movies.

Education

Many Negro leaders were convinced that still better educational opportunities would help the Negro cause. Although Booker T. Washington and W. E. B. Du Bois disagreed about the type of education that would be most helpful, they realized that both the skills emphasized by Washington and the academics preferred by Du Bois were necessary to develop leadership.

Dr. Carter G. Woodson. This educator and historian wrote books on the history of the Negro race. No one knew better than

Carter Woodson how important education was to an individual. Born in Virginia in 1875, he had little chance to go to school. He would work as a coal miner to support himself and then attend school for as long a period as he could. This was a slow way to get an education, and Carter Woodson was twenty-two years old when he finished high school. After attending Berea College in Kentucky, he continued his studies at the University of Chicago and at Harvard, where he earned a Ph.D.

Dr. Woodson was interested in Negro history. He realized that few people were aware of Negro contributions to American life. He was deeply concerned about the lack of information available on the subject. In 1915, he founded the Organization for the Study of Negro Life and History. The purpose of the organization was to do careful research and write accurate accounts of Negro history, which had been largely neglected. He became an enthusiastic worker and wrote, singly and with others, many history books. Some of these are still used as textbooks in high schools and colleges. The importance of Negroes to the progress of our nation is set forth in *The Negro in Our History, Negro Makers of History,* and *The History of the Negro Church.* Some of Dr. Woodson's books were used as references in the preparation of this book.

Dr. Charles H. Wesley.   Another educator, author, and historian who shared Dr. Woodson's concern for publishing information about Negro history is Dr. Charles Wesley. These two historians worked as co-authors of some history books. Together they wrote *The Story of the Negro Retold* and *The Negro in Our History.*

Keenly interested in the contributions of Negroes, Dr. Wesley has continued to study and write about significant achievements. He is the author of such histories and biographies as *Negro Labor in the United States, Richard Allen: Apostle of Freedom,* and *The Negro in the Americas.*

Dr. Wesley has also had a long and distinguished career as an educator. Interested primarily in college education, he has worked to widen opportunities for Negroes to attend college. He taught at Howard University and, in time, became Dean of the Graduate School there. He later served as president of Wilberforce University and then became president of Central State College in Wilberforce, Ohio.

Mary McLeod Bethune. A school teacher, the builder of a school, a public speaker, a government administrator—Mary McLeod Bethune was all of these and much more. Her whole life was devoted to helping young people, and the way she chose was through education.

Mary McLeod was born in South Carolina, the fifteenth child in the family and the only one who was born free. Her parents were share croppers, and there was plenty of work, and love too, in Mary's young life. She wanted desperately to go to school, but there was no school for Negro children in the small community. Then opportunity came. A mission school was established five miles from the McLeod log cabin. For Mary, the longed-for chance to read came true. After two years, she could read the Bible through, and she had learned enough arithmetic to help her neighbors with their accounts.

Opportunity again had a strange way of singling out Mary McLeod. In faraway Denver, Colorado, a Quaker seamstress by the name of Mary Chrissman sent money to the American Missionary Board. The money was to be used to educate a worthy Negro girl, and Mary was chosen. Long afterward, Mary McLeod wrote about her feeling when she heard the good news on that wonderful day: "Oh, the joy of that glorious morning. . . . I was but a little girl groping for the light . . . and away off in Denver, Colorado, a poor dressmaker, sewing for her daily bread, heard my name and came to my assistance. . . . To me, her memory is sacred!" [4]

Mary McLeod was twelve years old when she went to Scotia Seminary in North Carolina. She remained for seven years, studying in the winter and working during the summer months to earn

[4] Helen Bailey, *Forty American Biographies* (New York: Harcourt, Brace and World, Inc., 1964), pp. 219–20.

money for necessities. After leaving Scotia, she went to Moody
Bible Institute in Chicago. She hoped to become a missionary to
Africa, but no appointment was given to her. So Mary McLeod
became a school teacher, starting her career in Sumter, South
Carolina. There she met and eventually married Albertus
Bethune; there her only child, Albert, was born.

When the family moved to Florida, Mary Bethune was troubled by the sight of children growing up in poverty and ignorance.
Remembering how much her education had meant to her own
life, she was determined to bring the advantages of education to
others. She would start a school. She went to Daytona Beach,
which had no school for Negro children. Mary Bethune had a
great deal of determination and very little money. With only
$1.50 in her pocket, she rented a four-room cottage which would
serve as the first school. She visited houses in the neighborhood
and gathered together her first class. There were five little girls
whose families would pay fifty cents a week for their education.
She rang doorbells asking for donations for the school and then
made chairs and desks out of packing boxes. She raised money
by baking pies to sell. She and her pupils combed the junk yards
for anything that was usable and could be repaired. After two
years, there were two hundred and fifty girls in the Bethune
School. Besides learning school subjects, the girls learned to sew
and cook. A choir was trained. The girls in the choir often sang
in hotels where tourists were spending the winter, and collections
after the concerts bought supplies for the school. As the school
enlarged, more buildings and greater financial help were needed.
Mary Bethune appeared before audiences and told others of her
work. Some wealthy individuals gave advice, time, and money to
improve her school. One such helpful person was James Gamble.
He contributed money for buildings, land, and supplies for the
school and served as the chairman of the board of trustees. The
Bethune School grew in size and influence. In 1923, it merged
with Cookman Institute, a nearby college for Negro boys. The
new institution was known as the Bethune-Cookman College.

The depression years of the 1930's opened new ways for Mrs. Bethune to help young people. One of the emergency agencies founded by President Franklin Roosevelt was the National Youth Administration. Mrs. Bethune was appointed to serve as the Director of the Negro Affairs Division of the NYA. Her work kept her in close contact with both President and Mrs. Roosevelt, and she won the admiration of them both. During the nine years that the NYA program was in operation, it helped 600,000 Negro students stay in school.

Mary McLeod Bethune died at Daytona Beach in 1955. The words of her last will were as inspiring as her life of service had been.

Will of Mary McLeod Bethune

MY LAST WILL AND TESTAMENT

Sometimes I ask myself if I have any legacy to leave. My worldly possessions are few. Yet, my experiences have been rich. From them I have distilled principles and policies in which I firmly believe. Perhaps in them there is something of value. So, as my life draws to a close, I will pass them on to Negroes everywhere in the hope that this philosophy may give them inspiration. Here, then, is my legacy:

I LEAVE YOU LOVE. Injuries quickly forgotten quickly pass away. Personally and racially, our enemies must be forgotten. Our aim must be to create a world of fellowship and justice where no man's color or religion is held against him. "Love thy neighbor" is a precept which could transform the world if it were universally practiced. It connotes brotherhood and to me, brotherhood of man is the noblest concept of all human relationships. Loving your neighbor means interracial, interreligious, and international.

I LEAVE YOU HOPE. Yesterday, our ancestors endured the degradation of slavery, yet they retained their dignity. Today, we direct our economic and political strength toward winning a more abundant and secure life. Tomorrow, a new Negro, unhindered by race taboos and shackles, will benefit from this striving and struggling.

I LEAVE YOU A THIRST FOR EDUCATION. More and more, Negroes are taking full advantage of hard-won opportunities for learning, and the educational level of the Negro population is at its highest point in history. We are making greater use of the privileges inherent in living in a democracy. Now that the barriers are crumbling everywhere, the Negro in America must be ever vigilant lest his forces be marshaled behind wrong causes and undemocratic movements. . . . He must not lend his support to any group that seeks to subvert democracy.

I LEAVE YOU FAITH. Faith is the first factor in a life devoted to service. Without faith, nothing is possible. With it, nothing is impossible. Faith in God is the greatest power but great faith, too, is faith in oneself. The faith of the American Negro in himself has grown immensely, and is still increasing. The measure of our progress as a race is in precise relation to the depth of the faith in our people held by our leaders.

I LEAVE YOU RACIAL DIGNITY. I want Negroes to maintain their human dignity at all costs. We, as Negroes, must recognize that we are the custodians as well as the heirs of a great civilization. As a race, we have given something to the world, and for this we are proud and fully conscious of our place in the total picture of mankind's development.

I LEAVE YOU A DESIRE TO LIVE HARMONIOUSLY WITH YOUR FELLOW MEN. The problem of color is world wide, on every continent. I appeal to all to recognize their common problems, and unite to solve them. So often our difficulties have made us supersensitive and truculent. I want to see my people conduct themselves in all relationships, fully conscious of their responsibilities and deeply aware of their heritage. We are a minority of fifteen million living side by side with a white majority of 177 million. We must learn to deal with people positively and on an individual basis.

I LEAVE YOU FINALLY A RESPONSIBILITY TO OUR YOUNG PEOPLE. Our children must never lose this zeal for building a better world. They must not be discouraged from aspiring to greatness, for they are to be the leaders of tomorrow. We have a powerful potential in our youth, and we must have the courage to change old ideas and practices so that we may direct their power toward good ends.

Faith, courage, brotherhood, dignity, ambition, responsibility—
these are needed today as never before. We must cultivate them and
use them as tools for our task of completing the establishment of
equality for the Negro. We must sharpen these tools in the struggle
that faces us and find new ways of using them. The Freedom Gates
are half ajar. We must pry them fully open.

If I have a legacy to leave my people, it is my philosophy of living
and serving. As I face tomorrow, I am content. I pray now that my
philosophy may be helpful to those who share my vision of a world
of peace.[5]

[5] Rackham Holt, *Mary McLeod Bethune* (Garden City, N.Y.: Doubleday and
Company, Inc., 1964), pp. 287–89.

Negroes and whites stand in line together for soup and bread.

The Depression and
World War II:
1929—1945

The carefree years of the 1920's ended abruptly in 1929. This was the year of the stock market crash. For most Americans the 1920's had been prosperous and exciting, but the effect of the stock market crash of 1929 was felt throughout the country and marked the beginning of the worst depression in our history.

The Great Depression

The depression affected the lives of millions of Americans. Factories shut down, and workers were out of jobs. Banks were forced to close, and people lost their life savings. Small businesses collapsed, causing still more unemployment and suffering. At the height of the depression, approximately fourteen million Americans were jobless. For those who were fortunate enough to have a job, any job, the wages were small. The people faced cold, hard hunger. Emergency kitchens and bread lines were set up to feed the jobless.

Negroes in the Depression

Negroes as a group suffered more than other Americans during the depression years. Even before the stock market crash, industry had been unsteady. Factories cut expenses by doing away with jobs that were not absolutely essential. Workers who had been on the job for the shortest time were the first to be dropped. The Negro worker often described his position as the last one hired and the first one fired. The number of Negroes without jobs compared with the total number of Negroes was from three to four times greater than the percentage of unemployed whites. The depression affected Negro farm workers as well as factory workers. Thousands of tenant farmers lost their jobs when planters were forced to plant and harvest less cotton and tobacco.

During the depression, men became desperate for work. There was keen competition for available jobs, and white workers were eager to get menial jobs that usually had gone to Negroes. Without money, or a chance to earn it, the jobless experienced such suffering that relief agencies had to provide them with food and other necessities. By 1935, one Negro out of every four was on relief. Working together in the early 1930's, the Negroes of St. Louis developed a Jobs-for-Negroes plan. They bought only from the stores that hired Negro workers. Businesses that hired no Negro help lost their Negro customers. Many places of business located in Negro districts found that it was more profitable to hire Negroes. The same plan was used successfully in other large cities.

Negro Voters

From the time of the Civil War, Negroes had cast their votes for the Republican Party, the party of Abraham Lincoln. Their bitter poverty during the depression turned them, as well as a lot of other Americans, to the Democratic Party and its promises of help. It pledged to bring relief from poverty and reforms against discrimination. Negroes began to support the Democratic Party.

In 1932, many Negro voters transferred their loyalty to the Democratic Party and to Franklin Roosevelt. In 1934, Arthur Mitchell,
a Negro candidate from Chicago, was elected to the United States
House of Representatives. He was the first Negro Democrat to
sit in Congress. In the presidential election of 1936, the majority
of Negro voters in large cities voted overwhelmingly for the re-
election of President Roosevelt. No longer could the Negro voter
be counted upon to cast a Republican vote according to tradition.
Since that time, both major political parties have been aware of
the strength of Negro votes.

Negroes and the New Deal

The great depression was a national crisis. Under President
Roosevelt, the federal government worked out emergency meas-
ures to pull the country out of its economic collapse. These meas-
ures are referred to as the New Deal. A program of relief and
public works was set into motion to provide work for the jobless.
One agency was the Public Works Administration, known as
PWA. Under PWA, the national government supplied money for
the building of such things as streets, bridges, schools, and other
public buildings. Thousands of jobs were created, and both
Negroes and whites had a chance to go back to work.

The Works Progress Administration, WPA, started projects for
many different kinds of workers who needed jobs. Artists, musicians, and writers were able to find jobs under WPA. Young men
who joined the Civilian Conservation Corps, or the CCC, were
put to work as foresters. The Tennessee Valley Authority, TVA,
undertook the gigantic task of developing the whole Tennessee
River Valley. Dams and electrical plants were built in the area.
Tenant farmers were given help in buying land by the Bankhead-
Jones Farm Tenant Act of 1937. In addition, the National Youth
Administration helped hundreds of thousands of young people
remain in school by supplying them with part-time jobs. Negroes
shared in all of these programs and took advantage of the opportunities that were offered.

Under President Roosevelt, Negroes with high qualifications were appointed as public officials. Advisory boards were needed to set standards and make rules for the new agencies. In these and other government departments, well-qualified Negroes filled important positions. Mary McLeod Bethune was the Director of the Division of Negro Affairs of the NYA. The brilliant lawyer William Hastie served as Assistant Solicitor in the Department of Interior. He eventually was appointed Judge of the United States Court of Appeals. Dr. Robert Weaver was the first Negro to be an advisor in the Department of the Interior. Dr. Weaver continued working in government agencies, and in 1961 he was appointed Administrator of the Housing and Home Finance Agency. In 1966, he became the first Negro to serve in the President's Cabinet. He was appointed by President Johnson as Secretary of the newly established Department of Housing and Urban Development.

By 1940, more than a hundred competent Negroes held responsible positions in the Roosevelt Administration. Sometimes known as Roosevelt's "Black Cabinet," these specialists and advisors served the Departments of the Interior, Commerce, Justice, Public Health, the Farm Security Administration, the Housing Authority, the National Youth Administration, and the CCC. Claude McKay, Richard Wright, Frank Yerby, Ralph Ellison, and John H. Johnson were all employed in the Federal Writers Project. The talents of individuals were not only recognized; they were also used to help solve the nation's problems.

World War II

The rise of dictators in Europe and Asia marked the beginning of military power that would again bring the countries of the world to war. In 1931, Japan marched into China, and four years later, Italy invaded Ethiopia. Then in 1938, the army of Germany took Austria in two days, meeting little resistance. When Germany's Nazi army invaded Poland in 1939, Great Britain and France declared war on Germany.

The United States watched these developments with growing alarm. The strength of the German army caused the rapid defeat of many small countries. It was clear that even the strong European nations would have to fight for survival. The political democracy of the United States was gravely threatened. Even though our country was not at war, it took immediate steps to prepare for defense. Land, sea, and air forces were strengthened, and industries turned to the manufacturing of war supplies. Our nation became the arsenal for democracy, preparing for our own military strength and making war supplies available to other democracies.

Industry

By 1940, industry in the United States was expanding rapidly. Factories already in existence had speeded up production. New plants were opened to manufacture airplanes, ships, jeeps, tanks, and other arms. Many of these plants operated night and day around the clock, using three shifts of workers to keep production moving. In spite of a heavy demand for skilled workers, racial discrimination barred Negroes from getting jobs in certain defense industries. Unlike other workers who could appeal to labor unions, Negroes had been excluded from most of the labor unions themselves. Organizations like the Urban League and the NAACP did what they could to overcome racial discrimination in industry.

A. Philip Randolph.   A dramatic protest against such discrimination was planned by Asa Philip Randolph, a highly successful labor leader. During his lifetime, he has fought continually for improved working conditions and higher wages for Negro workers. When Negroes were kept out of most labor unions, Randolph worked to organize a union for Pullman porters. His efforts were successful when the Brotherhood of Sleeping-Car Porters came into existence in 1925. Later, Philip Randolph became vice-presi-

A. Philip Randolph

dent of the AFL-CIO. He also wrote articles for *Opportunity,* the magazine of the Urban League. Randolph remains an influential Negro leader today.

Willard Saxby Townsend.   Coming from humble origins in Cincinnati, Willard Saxby Townsend was another influential labor leader. He organized the redcaps of the city into a local union and later into a national union with headquarters in Chicago. Townsend was elected a vice-president of the CIO and was also the first Negro to be elected to the Executive Council of the merged AFL-CIO.

A March on Washington.   In 1941, Philip Randolph proposed to strike out against discrimination in industry. Believing that in union there is strength, he and other Negro leaders started plans for a mass march on Washington, D.C. The march would show dramatically that Negroes were displeased with the lack of equal job opportunities. Plans for the march came at a time when the country was already filled with tension because of the threat of war. President Roosevelt moved quickly to prevent the march by conferring with Randolph and other leaders of the plan. The result of the conference was the Executive Order 8802, which was issued on June 25, 1941. This document discouraged racial discrimination in defense plants.

Executive Order 8802.   This important order sought to "encourage full participation in the National Defense Program by all citizens of the United States, regardless of race, creed, color, or national origin, in the firm belief that the democratic way of life within the nation can be defended successfully only with the help and support of all groups within our borders." Because of the order, any industry that held a government contract had to hire qualified workers of any race. At the same time, the Fair Employment Practices Committee was appointed. The work of this committee was to investigate and solve charges of discrimination.

After the executive order, Negroes found it easier to get highly skilled jobs for which they received high wages. Because the workers of most defense plants were unionized, Negroes joined labor unions in large numbers. Their union membership gave them protection and backing in their struggle for better jobs. Other Negroes filled positions under federal civil service, and many entered professional and clerical work.

Participation in World War II

Even before the United States entered the war in 1941, the armed forces were being enlarged. The Selective Service Act was passed in 1940, and recruits were selected for military service.

During the war, over a million Negro men served in our country's defense. ⁄

Desegregation of the Armed Forces.   At the outbreak of the war, Negro servicemen trained and fought in all-Negro units. Since the policy of segregated fighting units had been used successfully in former wars, military leaders thought it was wise to follow the same pattern. Negro leaders and the Negro press criticized segregation in the armed forces, but it continued.

As the war progressed, steps were taken to break down segregation. Changes in the United States Navy show how racial barriers were overcome in this branch of the service. On Pearl Harbor Day, December 7, 1941, Negro servicemen were on battleships that were attacked by Japanese planes. Negroes were permitted only limited service in the Navy at that time; they served only as messmen. By 1942, Negroes were accepted as crewmen. They received their training in segregated camps and were assigned mainly to harbor ships. Two years later, a number of Negro crewmen were placed on twenty-five regular naval vessels on a trial basis. This experiment in integration worked smoothly and paved the way for other steps. In 1945, segregated training camps were closed, and, in February 1946, complete integration was achieved. Men were assigned to duty according to their qualifications, regardless of race or color.

Other branches of the armed services worked out plans to do away with racial discrimination. The merchant marine commissioned four Negroes as captains of Liberty Ships, and fourteen Liberty Ships were named for outstanding Negro individuals. In 1944, the Army faced a crisis which forced the immediate use of Negro and white troops fighting together. The Battle of the Bulge threatened to give victory to the German troops. Both Negro and white reinforcements were rushed to the combat scene.

The courage and effectiveness of Negro troops were recognized in all theaters of the war: in Europe, in the Mediterranean region, and in the South Pacific. In 1948, President Truman issued Executive Order 9981 which called for an official desegregation of the armed forces. Today in all branches of military service, Negro and white troops serve in the same units.

Negro Heroes.   For the United States, World War II began at Pearl Harbor on December 7, 1941. On that day, a young Navy messman, Dorie Miller, became one of the first heroes of the war. He had volunteered for service at Waco, Texas, when he was only nineteen years old. When he enlisted, he told the recruiting officer, "I'm gonna be a good sailor." And Dorie Miller was.

Dorie Miller was assigned to the battleship *Arizona,* which was stationed at Pearl Harbor on December 7. On that day, he and other crew members were startled by a sudden explosion. They saw a swarm of unfamiliar planes flying in fighting formation over the United States fleet. Miller saw the planes dive toward the *Arizona,* strafing the ship with gunfire as they came. Noticing that the captain lay wounded on the bridge, Dorie Miller went to his aid. The young sailor carried the captain below decks where he received medical attention. Still the enemy bombers came. Miller next turned to the defense of his ship. He saw one of the machine gunners fall at his station. Even though Dorie Miller, as a messman, had never received training in the use of a machine gun, he made his way to one of the ship's guns. Under fire, he took aim and scored direct hits upon four of the Japanese planes. For this heroic action. Dorie Miller was awarded the Navy Cross by President Roosevelt. The award was presented to him by Admiral Nimitz on June 10, 1942.

During a furlough, Dorie Miller enjoyed a hero's welcome at home. After further training, he was assigned to another vessel, the *Liscome Bay.* His new term of service was short. On November 24, 1942, the *Liscome Bay* suffered a direct hit by a submarine torpedo. Dorie Miller and many other crewmen and officers were lost at sea.

Colonel Benjamin O. Davis, Jr., a graduate of West Point, served in the Air Corps with great success. He commanded the 99th Fighter Squadron which flew many missions into Germany. Later, four squadrons united into one Air Force group, the

332nd Fighter Group. Colonel Davis commanded this all-Negro group, which continued air raids against the enemy in Europe. In 1945, the entire 332nd Group received a Unit Citation for distinguished service. Colonel Davis himself was awarded the Legion of Merit Award, the Silver Star, the Distinguished Flying Cross, and the Air Medal with four Oak Leaf Clusters.

After the war, Colonel Davis became commanding officer of Godman Field, the first Negro to be appointed as commander of an Army air base. He rose in rank to major general as he continued his service in the Air Corps. In 1965, he was promoted to the rank of lieutenant general, the highest rank ever held by a Negro in the United States armed forces. He was also appointed chief of staff of the armed forces in Korea.

Two Notable Contributors

Dr. Charles Drew.   A doctor and scientist, Charles Drew developed a process of changing blood into plasma. This important scientific discovery saved hundreds of thousands of lives during World War II.

He was born in Washington, D.C., in 1904. His natural ability in sports was shown at an early age for he won a swimming tournament when he was only eight years old. In high school he was a good student and a star athlete. He played on the football, basketball, and baseball teams and had an outstanding record in track. He then attended Amherst College in Massachusetts where he continued earning high grades and athletic honors. He was a member of the football and track teams. In 1924, he won an All-American mention as a half-back on the eastern football team. At his graduation from college, he was awarded a trophy as the student who had brought the greatest honor to his college during the four years of his attendance.

After a year of teaching at Morgan College in Baltimore, Charles Drew returned to college to study medicine. In spite of the difficult course of study, he continued to take part in athletics. Charles Drew seemed to excel in each of his chosen activities, becoming an outstanding doctor. In addition to his medical practice, he was a professor at Howard University and a surgeon at Freedmen's Hospital in Washington, D.C. In 1938, he went to Columbia University to study more surgery. While at Columbia, he worked on an important project of "banked blood." The world was ready for his work. Europe was already involved in World War II, and one important treatment for the wounded was to replace blood through life-giving transfusions.

Great Britain was the first country to use Dr. Drew's experience in preserving blood plasma for blood banks. He was asked to take charge of a blood plasma collection service so that large amounts of plasma would be available to British hospitals. In 1940, he became the medical supervisor of the Blood Transfusion Association. The following year he was appointed director of the Red Cross Blood Bank in New York City. He organized a large-scale collection of blood plasma for the armed forces of the United States.

The brilliant career of Dr. Charles Drew ended abruptly in 1950 when he was killed in an automobile accident. His research in the use of blood plasma saved countless lives, and plasma continues to save lives throughout the world.

Dr. Ralph Bunche.   After World War II, Dr. Ralph Bunche became world famous for his efforts in promoting peace. He was awarded the Nobel Peace Prize in 1950 for working out a truce between the Arabs and the Israelis in the Middle East. Each year since 1901, the Nobel prize has been awarded to some outstanding group or individual of the world who has worked for peace. Before 1950, only ten other American citizens had received this honor.

Ralph Bunche was well prepared to give noteworthy service. He had been a brilliant student, graduating from Los Angeles Jefferson High School as valedictorian of his class. He was a student at five different colleges. He was first graduated from the University of California with the highest honors in scholarship. He attended Harvard University where he received a Ph.D. degree. He then took additional work at Northwestern University

Dr. Ralph Bunche accepts the 1950 Nobel Peace Prize.

in Chicago, the London School of Economics, and the University of Capetown in South Africa. Dr. Bunche taught at Howard University where he was chairman of the Political Science Department.

His career in government service began in 1944 when he worked in the United States State Department. In 1946, he was appointed to serve in the United Nations as Director of the Division of Trusteeships. The United Nations was attempting to promote peace throughout the world. An explosive situation had arisen in Palestine. Fighting had broken out between the newly created country of Israel and the surrounding Arab states. With Dr. Bunche serving as peacemaker from the United Nations, an armistice was reached. War was averted.

Since 1950, Dr. Bunche has continued his work with the United Nations. He became Under Secretary of the United Nations in 1951 and then Under Secretary for Special Political Affairs in the United Nations Secretariat in 1958. During his career, he has received forty honorary degrees from different colleges and universities, a proof of the high respect in which he is held.

Dr. Bunche has always been interested in young people. In one interview, he gave the following suggestions for a happy and useful life: "To sum up, I would say to all youth everywhere, . . . broaden your interest; work hard and courageously; learn to like people, and to have faith in people; look on the bright side of life. Above all, have confidence in yourself and in the strength that comes from belief in a Supreme Being." [1]

[1] *Our Wonderful World* Encyclopedia, Vol. 4 (Chicago: Spencer Press, Inc., 1955), p. 416.

Leaders of the civil rights march lock arms in Washington, 1963.

The Search for Equality
1945−1966

War years are always times of crisis for any nation. In all the wars in which the United States took part, the best efforts of every citizen were needed. Negro soldiers, as well as white, had served courageously in every United States war. In World War II, however, greater opportunities for equal service were opened. Executive orders had abolished racial discrimination in defense plants and in the armed services. During the war years, Negroes and other citizens had worked closely together, sharing dangers and hardships. In many cases, these experiences resulted in better understanding and respect between the races.

The cause of this war emphasized our nation's belief in human rights. The United States and her allies, with the exception of the Soviet Union, were countries with political democracies. They opposed dictatorships where the rights of citizens were not protected. Even after the defeat of Japan, Nazi Germany, and Fascist Italy, dictatorships did not disappear. Communism, though it was supposed to be a new kind of democracy, grew into a dictatorship and spread, gaining in strength, until the nations of the world were divided again between democracy and dictatorship. The United States emerged from the war as the world leader of free nations. In the years of the cold war since 1945, the struggle against Communism has brought attention to the importance of human rights and freedom for all citizens. The protection of the rights of all minority groups is necessary for a strong democracy.

There was another factor which speeded progress toward equality after the war. Negroes, themselves, were in a stronger position to demand justice and to make their demands heard. After World War II, the Negro population was concentrated mainly in the large cities of the United States. The migration to the northern cities which had begun in the early 1900's had continued steadily thereafter. Population studies over a fifty-year period show a dramatic change from rural to urban living. In 1910, before the Negro migration began, 73 percent of the American Negroes lived on farms or in small cities of less than 2,500 persons. In 1960, just fifty years later, the picture had completely reversed. According to the 1960 census, 73 percent of the Negro population lived in large cities. At present, the percentage of Negroes living in cities is greater than that of whites.

The Negro's position was further strengthened by his service experience in World War II. The demands of citizens who had fought for an American victory abroad could not be ignored.

The growing industrialization of the United States also added strength to the Negro protest. Employed in various defense industries during the war, many Negroes filled positions of responsibility and earned higher wages. Even greater opportunities in industry were made available after the war. With higher wages, Negroes, as a group, increased their purchasing power in the industrial market. Today, approximately twenty million Negroes in the United States have a purchasing power of twenty-two billion dollars.

Urbanization, industrialization, and war service changed the lives of most Americans. For the Negro, these three developments produced an era in which the protest against injustice could take hold and become strong.

Toward Negro Advancement

Negro groups became more active in speaking out against discrimination and in trying to stop it. Established organizations like the NAACP and the Urban League increased their efforts while new groups and organizations were formed. There was an urgency for achieving immediate progress. By the 1960's, many workers for equal rights were saying, "Now is the time."

The NAACP

In the 1930's and 1940's, the NAACP had stepped up its drive for racial equality under the leadership of Walter White. The organization worked in two ways: to protect rights that had been guaranteed by law and to work for new laws that would bring greater equality. The NAACP was concerned with improving voting opportunities. It campaigned firmly against poll taxes. It also acted against racial violence, lynchings, and beatings. Walter White, himself, investigated the causes and results of mob violence. His accounts of such happenings helped influence public opinion against violence. The greatest success of the NAACP was its work in overcoming discrimination in education. Realizing the importance of the best possible education for all citizens, the association worked first to improve unequal conditions that existed. Through legal action, it won equal pay for Negro teachers in the South.

The NAACP continued its emphasis on education after the war. Thurgood Marshall, an outstanding lawyer who had received his training at Howard University Law School, became the chief legal counsel for the association. He once said he had always worked for justice for all people, regardless of race, creed, or color. His success in advancing Negro opportunities earned for him the nickname of "Mr. Civil Rights." In his work with the NAACP, Thurgood Marshall brought to court many cases that involved racial segregation in the public schools. At first, he did not question the separate-but-equal policy of the South. Nor did

Thurgood Marshall

he challenge the two school systems—one for white and the other for Negro pupils. His first efforts were concentrated on proving that the separate facilities were not equal. Therefore, his early cases dealt with situations where equality did not exist. Then in the 1950's, he worked on a case which challenged the separate-but-equal theory in public education. In 1952, the NAACP brought before the Supreme Court of the United States the case of *Brown vs. the Board of Education of Topeka.*

Brown vs. the Board of Education

In this well-known case, the Supreme Court was asked to make a decision about racially segregated schools. Each school district in the South had two school systems, one for Negro pupils and the other for white. Each of the school systems was required by law to have equally good facilities: buildings, supplies, and competent teachers. In actual practice, Negro schools were usually inferior. The *Brown vs. the Board of Education* case raised the question as to whether segregated schools, even if they were equal, deprived children of equal educational opportunities. After months of careful study, the Court reached its decision in 1954. All the Justices were agreed that segregated educational systems were unequal. In delivering the opinion of the Court, Chief Justice Warren emphasized the importance of education in today's world. He said, "Today, education is perhaps the most important function of state and local governments. . . . It is the very foundation of good citizenship. . . . In these days, it is doubtful that any child may reasonably be expected to succeed in life if he is denied the opportunity of an education. Such an opportunity . . . is a right which must be made available to all on equal terms."

Then the Chief Justice gave the opinion of the Court concerning the effect of segregation. He stated, "To separate (pupils) from others . . . solely because of their race generates a feeling of inferiority as to their status in the community that may affect their hearts and minds in a way unlikely ever to be undone." [1]

This important decision by the Supreme Court reversed the separate-but-equal policy that had been established in 1896 by the *Plessy vs. Ferguson* case. School districts that had segregated school systems were told by the Court to abolish segregation with "all deliberate speed."

In 1956, the Supreme Court extended the ban against segregation in education. It ruled that state universities and colleges, which were supported by the taxes of all citizens, should be open to all students.

The South faced a real problem in carrying out the orders of the Supreme Court. Habits and customs that have been followed for many years can be difficult to change rapidly. Realizing some of the difficulties involved, the Supreme Court permitted each school system to work out its own timetable for desegregation.

[1] Joseph Tussman, editor, *The Supreme Court on Racial Discrimination* (New York: Oxford University Press, 1963), pp. 40–41.

In some communities, there was bitter opposition to the integration order. Little Rock, Arkansas, erupted into mob violence in 1957, when nine Negro students registered for classes at the all-white Central High School. Federal troops were called out to maintain peace and to escort the pupils to their classes. Despite the fact that disorder continued for over a year, integration of schools continued. By 1962 the high schools in Little Rock had both Negro and white pupils. Southern colleges also faced the test of desegregation. Bitterness and violence occurred in Oxford, Mississippi, when James Meredith enrolled for classes at the University of Mississippi in 1962. Federal troops were again used to back up the ruling of the Supreme Court. Meredith attended classes with the protection of United States soldiers.

On the other hand, there were many southern communities which worked sincerely to bring about a trouble-free period of integration. Washington, D.C., started in 1955 to reorganize its schools without racial segregation. Plans for desegregation were carried out smoothly in West Virginia, Missouri, Texas, and Kentucky. In 1956, there were more than five hundred Negro students attending classes in southern colleges that had formerly had only white students. Since the Supreme Court decision, many southern colleges that are not tax-supported have also enrolled students on a nonracial basis.

The Intensification of the Protest Movement

The official order for desegregation in education was a step toward greater equality. At the same time, a growing resentment against other areas of discrimination gained strength in the South and spread to the North. No longer was there passive acceptance of segregation in transportation, hotels, restaurants, and other public buildings. Protests arose against unfair customs of keeping qualified Negroes from holding certain jobs because of race. The struggle for equality gained momentum, and unequal voting privileges and segregated housing were both sharply challenged.

In their quest for unlimited participation in all areas of American life, Negroes were joined by whites, and both races worked together in a crusade for equal rights. Rallying to the upsurge of the civil rights movement, thousands of individuals became actively involved in fighting against prejudice and discrimination. Each success in defeating one phase of discrimination resulted in determined efforts to attack another. Leaders in the struggle for equality indicated that there would be no turning back. They stated that as long as prejudice existed, it would be challenged.

After World War II, new organizations were formed to work for equal rights. These organizations used new methods to protest against discrimination and to force an immediate change. Mass demonstrations, picketing, and nonviolent resistance gave publicity to conditions of discrimination. Members of these organizations had a firm belief in their cause. In their struggle for equality, they faced many obstacles: insults, jail, and physical danger.

Some of the newly formed organizations challenged laws that upheld discrimination. The idea of achieving justice became more important than following unjust laws. If a law was considered unjust, then civil rights workers were urged to break the law in a nonviolent manner. This type of action is known as civil disobedience. When workers for equal rights sat at a segregated lunch counter, they were breaking a law which they felt was unjust. Marching without a parade permit was also a breach of law in many communities. In spite of threats of lawsuits, fines, or jail, members of some organizations continued to use civil disobedience as a form of protest against injustice.

This form of protest has been viewed with great concern by many people who wonder about its far-reaching effects. Does an individual citizen have the right to judge whether or not a law is unjust? Would the practice of disobeying some laws lead to a general disrespect for all laws and law-enforcing officers? What would happen if lots of people decided to break laws which they judged for themselves to be unjust? Could this form of protest flame into uncontrolled mob violence? Questions like these did not necessarily show disapproval of the civil rights movement.

Rather, they expressed a feeling that protest against injustice should be made within the existing legal framework.

The Montgomery Improvement Association

This group was formed to protest against racial segregation on city buses in Montgomery, Alabama. On December 1, 1955, Mrs. Rosa Parks was rudely ordered to give up her seat to a white man and move to the back of the bus. When she refused to do so, she was arrested. The incident came to the attention of Dr. Martin Luther King, Jr., an outstanding minister of the community. Dr. King led the way in forming the Montgomery Improvement Association to organize Negroes for action. The association set up an effective boycott against the bus company, and 98 percent of the Montgomery Negroes either walked to work or rode in car pools. The boycott was to continue until the bus company made two changes. It was to permit nonsegregated seating on buses and to employ Negro drivers on bus routes in Negro sections of the city. This was an effective protest, for Negroes made up more than half of the usual bus passengers. As the "Walk, Don't Ride" boycott continued, Martin Luther King, Jr., and other leaders of the Montgomery Improvement Association were arrested in February. The men were convicted of illegal boycotting but their convictions were overruled by a higher court. On November 13, 1956, the Supreme Court of the United States ruled that racial segregation was illegal on local public transportation. The following month, after a year of boycott, the Montgomery bus line began operating on a nonsegregated basis. The boycott itself did not bring an end to segregation. The ruling of the Supreme Court brought the power of the law to put an end to segregation on public transportation.

Dr. Martin Luther King, Jr.   The success of the Montgomery Improvement Association brought attention to the leadership of Martin Luther King, Jr., and his tremendous influence over Negroes in the South. Born in 1929 in Atlanta, Georgia, he was named Michael Lewis King. His father was a minister. When he told his young son about the courageous life of Martin Luther, the boy adopted this name as his own. After high school, Martin Luther King, Jr., attended Morehouse College in Atlanta. While there, he decided to become a minister. He went to graduate school at Crozer Theological Seminary in Pennsylvania where he received recognition for outstanding scholarship. From there, he went to Boston University where he earned a Ph.D. degree in philosophy. Dr. King then returned to the South and became the minister of the Dexter Avenue Baptist Church in Montgomery, Alabama.

His religious background and knowledge of philosophy convinced Martin Luther King, Jr., that love and nonviolence have great power. He has often stated that hatred harms the person who hates just as much as the one who is hated. He has told his followers, "Let no man drag you so low as to hate." [2]

As a leader he has been concerned with using a powerful weapon against injustice. This technique is mass action in a nonviolent manner. Great numbers of people have joined in demonstrations to bring reforms. Demonstrations were carefully planned; the goals for which the group was working were clear cut; and members were trained to meet any possible violence without fighting back.

After the Montgomery success, Dr. King led another group, the Southern Christian Leadship Conference, SCLC. This organization, formed in 1957, worked to overcome segregation on city buses in other communities.

The most severe test of the power of Dr. King's nonviolent resistance was made in Birmingham, Alabama, in 1963. He stated that Birmingham was the most thoroughly segregated big city in the United States. He and other leaders planned huge demonstrations against segregation. The demonstrations aimed at three goals: first, to desegregate lunch counters, rest rooms, and drinking fountains in department stores; second, to provide more and better jobs for competent Negroes; and third, to create a com-

[2] Russell Adams, *Great Negroes Past and Present* (Chicago: Afro-Am Publishing Company, Inc., 1964), p. 106.

mittee of white and Negro leaders to work together on other plans for desegregation.

In April, the demonstration got under way and the marching began. The demonstrators were met with determined resistance. In the violence that followed, worldwide publicity was given to the Negro's cause. Public opinion was strongly on the side of the Negro. Nothing stopped the determined demonstrators. By May, a settlement was reached. Birmingham community leaders met with civil rights leaders to work out solutions for immediate problems. Plans were also made for future improvements.

Martin Luther King, Jr., continued to give leadership in the fight against segregation in other communities. He has pointed out that nonviolent resistance is effective only when it is carefully planned and focused on getting rid of one specific injustice at a time. When demonstrations or boycotts have been used unwisely, they have resulted in criticism and antagonism. Worse than that, they have lost friends for the Negro and his cause. Dr. King has declared that the campaign for equal rights will continue as long as any form of racial segregation exists.

In 1964, Dr. Martin Luther King, Jr., was awarded the Nobel Peace Prize. He was the second American Negro to receive this honor, following Dr. Ralph Bunche.

Dr. Martin Luther King is congratulated for his Nobel Peace Prize, 1964.

The Student Non-Violent Coordinating
Committee (SNCC)

Four college students at Greensboro, North Carolina, provided the inspiration for this organization. In February of 1960, the four young Negroes sat at a segregated lunch counter in a department store and waited for service. They were ignored, but they remained at the lunch counter until the store closed. This started the sit-in type of protest which spread to many communities throughout the South. College students formed their own organization, the Student Non-Violent Coordinating Committee. Both white and Negro students from many colleges became involved.

Youths support SNCC sit-ins in the South at a counter in New York.

They took part in "read-ins" in segregated libraries, "wade-ins" in segregated swimming pools, and "kneel-ins" in segregated churches. They were often jailed, fined, and sentenced to gang work, but as a result of the widespread sit-in movement, desegregation of many public facilities occurred.

In 1964, SNCC spearheaded in Mississippi a "Freedom Summer" project in which student volunteers from all over the country set up schools and voter registration centers. In 1966, Stokely Carmichael became Chairman of SNCC. Carmichael, then 24, fostered the much-disputed slogan "black power" and swung the organization to a more assertive philosophy, urging Negroes not to depend on whites for help.

The Congress of Racial Equality (CORE)

This organization was formed during the war years in 1942. Founded by James Farmer, CORE soon became a national organization. Its main office was in New York City, and branches were opened in other large cities in the United States.

In 1961, CORE repeated a unique nonviolent technique that its members had first used in 1947. To strike a blow against segregation on interstate buses, CORE sent out "freedom riders" who ignored rules about segregation. In the late 1940's, little attention had been paid to the experiment. By 1961, however, times had changed. With national interest focused on the struggle for equal rights, the "freedom rider" technique was more effective. "Freedom riders," both Negro and white, sat side by side on buses. They defied segregation of facilities in bus stations. Negro and white travelers sat together in segregated waiting rooms. They bought tickets together at segregated ticket windows and ate together at lunch counters. In the majority of southern states, little difficulty was met. In Alabama, however, the freedom riders were faced with violent opposition. Though this freedom ride was called off, others continued through 1961 and part of 1962. Publicity given to this project built favorable support for the freedom riders. By the end of 1962, desegregation in bus seating and in station facilities had been accomplished in many communities.

Floyd McKissick, National Director of CORE since 1965, has pointed out that the phrase "black power" carries the implication that Negroes do not yet have as much political power as their numbers warrant. He has urged political and economic action, suggesting the formation of a Negro political party.

The Nation of Islam

The most militant group in the protest movement is the Nation of Islam, more popularly called the Black Muslims. This group was started in Detroit in 1930, in the midst of the Depression, by W. D. Fard who preached about the beliefs of Islam. In sections of Africa from which slaves were brought to America, there had been an Islamic culture, and at least a few of the Negroes captured as slaves had been Moslems, or Muslims. Fard urged his followers to work for a complete separation of Negroes and whites.

The leadership of this group was taken over by Elijah Muhammad, born Elijah Poole in rural Georgia. Poole met Fard in Detroit, worked with him there until 1934, and then took over the movement. The Black Muslims dropped their last names and took on the letter X to indicate that their true names had been lost during slavery. Their program stressed racial pride, honesty, thrift, cleanliness, and hard work. They established separate parochial schools, opened all-Negro businesses, and mosques. They expressed contempt for Christianity, the Caucasian race, and for Negro leaders who worked for integration. With the aid of his sons and of a young follower, Malcolm X, Muhammad transformed the Black Muslims from a small cult in the slums of Detroit to an elaborate national organization.

In 1964 Malcolm X broke with Muhammad and set up his own movement, the Organization of Afro-American Unity, which also supported separation of races and violence. Malcolm's beliefs were changing towards a more moderate position when he was silenced by assassination in 1965, as he delivered a speech to his followers in New York.

The March on Washington

The struggle for equal rights reached one climax in the summer of 1963. A March on Washington was planned. One of its leaders was the same A. Philip Randolph who had organized the threatened march in 1941. Citizens who joined the march expressed their wish for greater racial equality. On August 28, the marchers assembled in Washington. They came from every section of the country, two hundred thousand of them. There were Negro and white marchers. They moved in an orderly fashion from the Washington Monument to the Lincoln Memorial where they listened to speeches by Negro leaders. It was here that Dr. Martin Luther King, Jr., expressed his hopes for the future of his race and his country. He said, "I have a dream that one day, on the red hills of Georgia, sons of former slaves and the sons of former slave holders will be able to sit down together at the table of brotherhood . . .

"I have a dream that my little children will one day live in a nation where they will not be judged by the color of their skin but by the content of their character."

Events and Legislation: 1964, 1965, and 1966

Civil rights is a term which is used to describe the rights of citizens. Leaders in the United States who work for civil rights have felt that American citizens of all races should have equal rights.

One problem in reaching racial equality was the fact that each state had different laws. Some state laws encouraged racial discrimination. Civil rights workers felt a national law was needed to protect the rights of all citizens. In 1963, President John F. Kennedy called for a national civil rights law. When Lyndon B. Johnson became president after the death of President Kennedy, he also declared the need for a national law on civil rights.

Civil Rights Act, 1964

In June, 1964, Congress passed the Civil Rights Act, which became the law of the land. The new law abolished racial discrimination in four situations. First, all citizens had equal rights to use facilities that were paid for by taxes. Examples of such facilities are parks, libraries, some hospitals, schools, and playgrounds. Second, discrimination was banned in most business places which served the public: stores, theaters, restaurants, and hotels, for example. Third, the Civil Rights Act granted equal voting rights for all citizens. States could still require voters to pass certain tests before they would be permitted to vote, but the same test would have to be given to all voters. Finally, the Civil Rights Act banned discrimination in employment and in union membership.

The Civil Rights Act was a national law that would be followed in all sections of the country. It guaranteed many of the opportunities for which organizations had been working. It opened wider opportunities for better jobs, for greater participation in voting, and for the use of public facilities.

During the summer that followed the passage of the 1964 Civil Rights Act in June, violence and unrest increased. Among Negroes, there were riots in New York, Philadelphia, Chicago, and New Jersey. In July three civil rights workers were murdered. A federal grand jury in Mississippi indicted eighteen white men for conspiracy in the slayings, but the U.S. District Judge who heard the case dismissed the charges on the grounds that the case came under state, not federal jurisdiction. Seventeen of these men and two new men were named in February 1967, in new federal indictments for conspiracy to violate the victims' civil rights.

In March of 1965, Martin Luther King led a 54-mile hike from Selma to Montgomery, Alabama, to dramatize the need for Negro voting registration in the South. More than 3,200 people hiked 54 miles, but there were 24,000 whites and Negroes who gathered at the end of the march in front of the courthouse steps in Montgomery. A white civil rights worker from Michigan was shot and killed as she drove a Negro rights worker along a highway toward Selma. A man accused of the murder was tried and acquitted.

Voting Rights Act, 1965

When it was shown that some sections of the South were not granting equal voting opportunities, Congress passed a special law to guarantee this right. On August 6, 1965, the Voting Rights Act became law of the land. The law aimed a blow at literacy tests when they were used to keep Negroes from registering to vote. States or counties where less than half of the citizens of voting age were registered had to suspend the literacy test. In addition, the Voting Rights Act granted authority for federal agents to supervise the registration of voters in certain areas.

During the summer of 1965, a riot in Watts, the Negro section of Los Angeles, raged for six days, left some 35 people dead and over a thousand injured, and caused thousands of dollars of damage to property. These riots, on a smaller scale, were repeated in March, 1966.

In 1966 the number of Negroes registered as voters in the South was still low in comparison to the number of Negroes old enough to vote. James Meredith, the first Negro to enroll in the University of Mississippi, began an individual march from Memphis, Tennessee, to Jackson, Mississippi, to try to convince Ne-

On their way to Jackson, from the left: Dr. Martin Luther King, James Meredith, Stokely Carmichael, and Floyd McKissick.

groes along the route and elsewhere that they had nothing to fear from southern whites and should register to vote. Ironically, a southern white responded to this march by shooting and wounding Meredith as he walked along U.S. Highway 51. Meredith was temporarily hospitalized, and civil rights workers, Negro and white, from all over the country rushed to Mississippi to take up his walk. This gathering together of leaders in the protest movement brought to light what appears to be the widening gap between the more militant programs of SNCC and CORE and the moderates as represented by the NAACP and SCLC and the Urban League.

Negro Contributions to American Life

From the middle of the 1930's to the present time, Negroes have built successful careers in every field of American life. Better job opportunities in large cities resulted in higher wages and a higher standard of living for many Negro families. Educational opportunities had also increased, and college education was no longer beyond the reach of most ambitious students. In ever-increasing numbers, Negroes have entered professional occupations. Opportunities, both for training and for practice, have weakened some of the long-standing barriers of discrimination in the professions. The 1960 census shows the number of Negroes in certain professions and technical occupations and gives the percentage of Negroes compared to all other U.S. citizens in the same profession:

Occupations	Negro citizens in occupation	Percentage of total occupation
Accountants and auditors	3,662	.77
Architects	1,878	1.84
Clergymen	15,852	3.04
Lawyers and judges	2,180	1.02
Musicians and music teachers	9,305	4.84

Occupations	Negro citizens in occupation	Percentage of total occupation
Physicians and surgeons	4,706	2.05
Social scientists	2,059	2.07
Social welfare and recreation workers	14,276	10.72
Teachers	130,658	7.81
Medical and dental technicians	9,767	7.06
Dietitians and nutritionists (Women only)	3,507	14.46
Librarians (Women only)	3,144	4.37
Professional Nurses (Women only)	27,034	4.76

Higher standards of living and education are factors which have increased Negro interest and participation in the arts, sciences, and professions. Important, also, have been a greater acceptance and appreciation of Negro achievements by all Americans. Talented Negroes proved that they had the ability to excel in many professions. By doing so, they won a greater respect for themselves and their race.

Sports

In the sports world, there is an impressive list of Negro athletes who have won fame because of exceptional performance. Many of the individuals are still regarded as champions in their field. Their rise to success made them popular heroes of the day.

Track.   Perhaps because speed and distance are carefully measured, it is hard to discriminate against a track man, and track was the first major sport in which Negroes won wide recognition. Jesse Owens stands out as one of the greatest American athletes of all times. Born in Alabama, Jesse Owens moved to Cleveland, Ohio, with his family when he was still a boy. When he was in junior high school, he excelled in running and jumping. His track coaches in junior and senior high school encouraged his development by giving special training to their star athlete. At Ohio State University, he became a star.

In 1936, Jesse Owens was a member of the United States track team that played in the Olympic games. Since Berlin, Germany, was the host city for the Olympic games that year, the event attracted worldwide attention. Germany had recently come under the rule of Adolf Hitler, whose violent speeches against racial minority groups disturbed the world. This intolerance was apparent to the members of the United States Olympic team since the Negro athletes were treated with contempt.

It was here that Jesse Owens had his most spectacular success. He set three records in Olympic competition in the 100-meter dash, the 200-meter dash, and the broad jump. Hitler himself watched the superb performance of Jesse Owens as the world's fastest runner. But the dictator quickly left the stands before four gold medals were presented to the great American athlete. The fourth gold medal was for placing first in the 400-meter relay. Teamed with Owens and placing second behind him in the 400-meter relay of the Berlin Olympics was Ralph Metcalf. Negroes took seven gold medals that year.

Meredith Gourdine, an outstanding broad jumper from Harvard won a second place silver medal for broad jump in the 1952 Olympics at Helsinki. Gourdine is now an engineering physicist working under a government grant to devise cheaper means of generating electricity.

In the 1960 Olympics at Rome, three Negro track stars took gold medals. Wilma Rudolph, often called the world's speediest woman, won her three gold medals for the women's 100-meter and 200-meter runs and for the 400-meter relay. Miss Rudolph did not begin to run, even to walk, until the age of eight, being a victim of various crippling diseases in her earliest years. Rafer Johnson, set a world record to win the Decathlon at Rome. He is considered one of the greatest athletes on record. Ralph Boston picked up his gold medal at Rome for the broad jump. He placed second instead of first at the Tokyo Olympics in 1964, but is preparing for the 1968 Olympics in Mexico City.

In the 1964 Olympics, Bob Hayes won two gold medals, one for the 100-meter run and one for the 400-meter relay. The Na-

tional Academy of Sports voted him the outstanding male track
and field athlete of 1964. He went from track to football, playing
end for the Dallas Cowboys.

Joe Louis, after knocking out Max Schmeling, 1938.

Boxing. Boxing is a sport that has produced many Negro
champions. But none captured the public imagination or became
a popular hero as quickly as Joe Louis. His life story leads from
dire poverty to worldwide fame. Joe Louis Barrow was born in
Alabama in 1914 of parents who were sharecroppers. Like many
other rural families, the Barrows moved to Detroit to try to make
a better living. Joe Louis started working out in local gyms, and

in 1933 he won the heavyweight championship in the Detroit Golden Gloves tournament.

After that, he rose quickly in the boxing world. He was aiming for world championship and defeated a number of heavyweight boxers in his campaign to reach the top. One bout he lost. In 1936, he was knocked out by Max Schmeling, the German boxer, who later boasted about his victory over the "inferior Negro fighter." The world championship finally came to Joe Louis in 1937 when he defeated James Braddock for the title. He remained world champion for twelve years, longer than any other individual. During these years, he defended his title twenty-five times. One of the most dramatic fights was a rematch with Max Schmeling in 1938. It was one of the shortest fights in Louis's career. He knocked out the German fighter in the first round.

Joe Louis won the respect of his countrymen not only because of his boxing skill, but also because of his modesty and his sportsmanship. He demonstrated his patriotism by serving as a private in the Army. More than that, he donated his share of the earnings from two of his fights to Army and Navy relief. Asked why, Joe Louis replied, "I'm fighting for my country." [3] Joe Louis retired undefeated and was followed by such future Negro champions as Ezzard Charles, Sugar Ray Robinson, Floyd Patterson, Sonny Liston, and Cassius Clay.

Baseball. It was not until after World War II that Negro athletes had the chance to play in professional team sports. Jackie Robinson, the first Negro to play in major league baseball, succeeded on two counts. He made an excellent career for himself, and he led the way for other Negro athletes to play professional baseball. Although he had some unpleasant experiences with discrimination, his top-quality performance on the ball field won the respect of his teammates, of opposing teams, and of the baseball fans.

Even as a child, Jackie Robinson had been good at games. When he attended high school in Pasadena, California, he was

[3] Roi Ottley, *New World A-Coming* (Boston: Houghton Mifflin Company, 1943), p. 200.

a member of the football, basketball, baseball, and track teams. His interest in athletics continued when he went to college. In 1939 at UCLA, he was a well-known football star, and during the next two years he won recognition for his ability in basketball.

After college, Jackie Robinson joined the Army. He qualified for Officers' Candidate School, and after intensive training, he became a lieutenant. He remained in the Army until 1944.

Following his military service, young Jackie Robinson was faced with choosing a career. His chances in professional baseball were limited because he was a Negro. In 1944, major league teams were closed to Negro athletes, no matter how talented they were. Negro athletes played in segregated, all-Negro leagues with little chance to become nationally recognized. Jackie Robinson chose baseball anyway, and he played with the Kansas City Monarchs, an all-Negro team. His career seemed settled.

Changing attitudes toward the Negro after World War II brought changes to the sports world, too. Newspaper articles questioned racial segregation in the major leagues. Sports writers suggested that Negro players be given a chance to compete in the big leagues. Branch Rickey, president of the Brooklyn Dodgers, became interested in adding a Negro ballplayer to his organization. Because he realized that any Negro would probably meet discrimination on and off the ball field, Rickey wanted a player with character and intelligence, as well as athletic ability. When baseball scouts repeatedly mentioned Robinson's name as an outstanding player, Rickey checked on his background. Everything seemed in Robinson's favor: he had college training; he had played in sports competition with both Negro and white athletes; and he was a good ballplayer. Jackie Robinson was called in for an interview. After being offered the opportunity to join the Brooklyn organization, he was told very frankly of some unpleasant situations that he would probably face if he took the job. With the clear understanding that his success or failure would influence the future of other Negro ballplayers, Jackie Robinson signed a contract. On October 15, 1945, Branch Rickey made the startling announcement to the newspapers that Jackie Robinson, Negro

Jackie Robinson practicing for a Dodger-Yankee game, 1947.

ballplayer, would play regularly with the Dodger farm club, the Montreal Royals.

The choice of Jackie Robinson as a pioneer Negro in major league baseball was an excellent one. He met and refused to be upset by such unpleasant experiences as name calling, Jim Crow accommodations, and crank notes. His baseball record was impressive from the beginning. During his first year with Montreal, the Royals were first in the International League, and Robinson was their outstanding player. In his second year with Rickey, Jackie Robinson entered the big leagues by becoming the regular first baseman for the Brooklyn Dodgers. At the end of the season, he was voted the Rookie-of-the-Year. In 1947, he led the National League in stolen bases and even succeeded in stealing home on five different occasions. Later, as second baseman, his brilliant playing continued throughout his career with the Dodgers. He was twice honored with the Most Valuable Player of the Year Award. He retired in 1956, and became vice-president of a chain of restaurants in New York City and a vigorous spokesman for the NAACP.

Within a few years, Negroes were playing on every major league team. Twelve years after Jackie Robinson had paved the way, there were fifty-seven Negro major leaguers in both the National and American Leagues. Many became outstanding stars. Besides Jackie Robinson, the following Negro athletes have won the Most Valuable Player Award: Roy Campanella, Willie Mays, Don Newcombe, Hank Aaron, Ernie Banks, Frank Robinson, and Maury Wills.

Professional Basketball and Football. Professional basketball and football teams have also been strengthened by the outstanding performances of Negro players. The skill and speed of such players as Wilt Chamberlain, Elgin Baylor, and Oscar Robertson have brought loud cheers from basketball fans. In 1966, Bill Russell, star player for the Boston Celtics, was chosen to manage the team for the following season. This was another first: the first Negro manager of a professional team in organized sports. In professional football, "Night Train" Lane, Lenny Moore, Jimmy Brown, Bobby Mitchell, and Roosevelt Greer are just a few of the stars whose exploits are well known to sports fans.

Tennis.   Tennis, as a sport, has produced few Negro stars. Althea Gibson, who grew up in Harlem, was the first exceptional Negro performer in this sport. Growing up in the 1940's when national competition was closed to Negroes, she became champion of the American Tennis Association, composed largely, but not exclusively, of Negro players. In 1950, the color ban in tennis competition was relaxed. Althea played for the first time against other national tennis stars. In 1957, she reached the peak of her career, winning three important championships to become the world's best woman tennis player. She later wrote an autobiography, *I Wanted to Be Somebody.* She is.

Arthur Ashe, Jr., placed first in the South Australian Tennis Championship matches in December 1966, graduating that year from the University of California at Los Angeles. Two years earlier in 1964 Ashe was rated among the nation's top ten amateur players and was the first Negro to make the United States Davis Cup team. Born in Richmond, Virginia, Ashe was sponsored by Dr. Robert Johnson of that city and sent to St. Louis for his senior year in high school so that he could play in integrated tournaments. At the age of 17, he was the first Negro to win the United States Lawn Tennis Association's Interscholastic championship.

The Arts

The Harlem Renaissance had sparked Negro enthusiasm and participation in all the arts during the 1920's. The depression years which followed made it difficult for artists, musicians, and writers to work, but national programs like WPA gave the talented a chance to develop their creative abilities. Negro contributions to the arts continued through the 1940's, 50's, and 60's.

The Visual Arts.   Horace Pippin was a self-taught artist who overcame many obstacles in his rise to success. His family was poor. The future artist left school after the elementary grades to work in a number of menial jobs. He loved to draw and paint and took his sketching pad with him wherever he went. In World War I, he served overseas and was severely wounded. Upon his discharge from the Army, Horace Pippin received the French Croix de Guerre and the American Purple Heart.

Still interested in art, Horace Pippin found it hard to hold a paint brush in his hand. His war wound prevented him from raising his right hand as high as his shoulder. But he was determined to paint. At first he held a wooden board in his lap. With a hot poker he drew outlines for his pictures on it and then filled in the outlines with house paint. Gradually he recovered the use of his right arm and could paint on canvas with artist's paints. Although it took him three years to complete his first canvas, he continued with the work he loved. In 1940, he had a successful one-man art show in New York City. Four of his paintings were exhibited in the Museum of Modern Art in that city.

Charles White, born in Chicago, now lives in California where he has been involved in preaching, teaching, and art. His drawings are strong and moving. He portrays Negro personalities with fine draughtsmanship and great vitality.

Jacob Lawrence lives in New York City. He spent much of his free time in a neighborhood settlement house where he was encouraged to draw and paint. He studied at the American Artists' School in New York. Examples of his work come from his panels on Negro history: "The Life of Frederick Douglass," "The Life of Harriet Tubman," and "The Migration of the Negro."

Many other contemporary artists of note could be named, among them Hale Woodruff, John Biggers, and Philip Hampton.

Gordon Parks rose from poverty to become a successful photographer. Born on a small farm in Kansas in 1912, he moved to St. Paul, Minnesota, in his late teens. When he left high school, Parks worked at numerous jobs before choosing a career in photography in 1937. He then moved to Chicago, where he was encouraged by the artists at the South Side Community Art Center. He was given a dark room in which to work, and eventually held a one-man exhibit. Parks became a staff photographer for *Life* magazine in 1949, and was named "Magazine Photographer of the Year," in 1961. Parks has also composed several pieces of classical music, and has written a book on photography and a novel, *The Learning Tree*.

Music and Dancing. Negroes with musical talent followed careers on the concert stage and in the Metropolitan Opera Company. In the footsteps of Marian Anderson and Roland Hayes, a number of young singers achieved fame as serious musicians. Among them were Dorothy Maynor, Carol Bryce, Gloria Davy, William Warfield, and Leontyne Price. Even more recent arrivals are George Shirley, Grace Bumbry, and Shirley Verrett. André Watts, a pianist, has played with the New York Philharmonic Symphony and other nationally known orchestras.

Outstanding musical performance demands training. Each of the talented musicians who rose to fame had excellent musical training, either from well-known teachers or from conservatories of music. Each had also attended college before beginning a professional study of music. Most had received help from a sponsor who had both the wealth and interest in seeing a great talent developed.

William Warfield's life serves as an example of a young musician's progress toward achievement. He grew up in Rochester, New York, where his father was a minister. A good student, young Warfield was also liked by his classmates, who elected him vice-president of the student council. His voice already showed great promise during high school, and his music teacher gave him private voice lessons without charge. The whole community was proud of William Warfield's talents and predicted a bright future for him.

While still in high school, he was entered in a national contest sponsored by the Music Teachers' Association. The only Negro contestant, William Warfield emerged as the winner. The prize in the contest had a marked influence over his future. It was a full scholarship to the music conservatory of his choice. William Warfield attended the Eastman School of Music in Rochester.

After three years of military service, Warfield turned to music to earn a living. At first he worked in night clubs, singing all kinds of music from classical to jazz. When he was appearing in Toronto, Canada, his voice made a deep impression on a man in the audience. This man, Walter Carr, made arrangements for the young baritone to give a concert at Town Hall, and his musical career was launched.

Another singer, Leontyne Price, was born in Mississippi, earned a B.S. degree from Central State College in Wilberforce, Ohio, and studied at the Juilliard School of Music in New York. Her first success followed her singing of the role of Bess in the 1952 revival of *Porgy and Bess*. Renown in opera followed her singing of the lead in *Aïda* on a European tour in 1959. After that, she landed a starring role in the Metropolitan Opera's production of Verdi's *Il Trovatore* in 1961 and was named "Musician of the Year" by a group of editors and critics. The peak of her career, so far, came when she opened the new Metropolitan Opera House in New York, in 1966, singing the lead in Samuel Barber's new opera, *Antony and Cleopatra*. In 1964, she was one of thirty Americans receiving the Freedom Medal, the highest American civil honor.

In popular music the roster is full of famous names. The late Nat King Cole and the late Billie Holliday will long be noted for their singing of popular music and blues. Ella Fitzgerald, Harry Belafonte, Lena Horne, Pearl Bailey, Eartha Kitt, Sammy Davis, Jr., and The Supremes, Diana Ross, Mary Wilson, and Florence Ballard offer a wide range of talents and styles. Mahalia Jackson is probably the most famous of the gospel singers.

In the 1930's Negro jazz gained great popularity over the radio. Fletcher Henderson, Duke Ellington, and Count Basie played pianos and directed bands. The last two, as well as Louis Armstrong, Coleman Hawkins, Jelly Roll Morton, Earl Hines, and Dizzy Gillespie, on their various instruments, span the 1920's to the 1960's. Cool jazz, seldom danced to, as opposed to the older music, characterizes the most recent jazz, and familiar names are those of Miles Davis playing the trumpet, Charlie Mingus on

Justino Diaz and Leontyne Price as Antony and Cleopatra.

the bass, Thelonius Monk on the piano, and John Coltrane on the saxophone.

Arthur Mitchell of the New York City Ballet has won an international reputation in the field of dance. He is the first Negro to attain the distinction of becoming a leading dancer of one of the world's great ballet companies. Mitchell was encouraged to pursue his talent for the dance by a guidance teacher who urged him to enroll in the High School of the Performing Arts in New York. There, Mitchell majored in modern dance but decided to try classical ballet after being offered a scholarship to study at the School of American Ballet. Arthur Mitchell has devoted much of his spare time to work with Negro children in the hope of inspiring them to follow careers in ballet.

During the 1940's and 1950's Katherine Dunham was one of the nation's foremost dancers and choreographers. Pearl Primus was well known in the 1950's. Eleo Pomare and his dance company are becoming known in the 1960's.

Acting.   Ossie Davis and Ruby Dee are listed among the most versatile Negro actors. Sidney Poitier won an Academy Award as the best actor in 1963 for his performance in *Lilies of the Field.* Diahann Carroll starred in a successful Broadway musical, *No Strings,* in 1962. Gloria Foster has won acclaim for her role in New York productions of *In White America* and *Medea;* she is now a member of the repertory theatre at Lincoln Center, in New York.

Literature.   The success of Negro authors in the 1920's continued and grew in the years that followed. A whole new generation of authors began to gain recognition. Many of the young authors wrote from their own experience, and their works often dealt with racial themes. Richard Wright wrote powerful novels that protested against discrimination in American life. Arna Bontemps found success in different kinds of writing: history, fiction, poetry, and biography. Frank Yerby turned his back on the racial theme and wrote best-seller novels of swashbuckling adventure and romance, including *Foxes of Harrow,* which became a movie. Willard Motley gained prominence with his books, *Knock on Any Door,* 1947, and *Let No Man Write My Epitaph,* 1958.

Ralph Ellison won the National Book Award in 1953 for his novel *The Invisible Man.* The late Lorraine Hansberry wrote *Raisin in the Sun,* which ran on Broadway for a year beginning in 1959, was taken on a tour of the country, and eventually was made into a movie.

James Baldwin has spoken and written strongly for the protest movement with his *Nobody Knows My Name,* 1961, and *Fire Next Time,* 1963. His provocative play *Blues for Mr. Charlie* was written in 1964.

Gwendolyn Brooks is one of the noteworthy American poets of today. She is the only American Negro who has ever won the Pulitzer prize for excellence in writing. Her first volume of poetry, *A Street in Bronzeville,* received high praise from book reviewers. *Annie Allen,* her second book, was awarded the Pulitzer prize for poetry.

Science

Among today's Negro scientists is Percy Julian, whose work in chemical research has brought him recognition and wealth. His life story is a dramatic example of the progress that has been made by one Negro family in just three generations. Percy Julian's grandfather was a slave, who was punished severely for learning to read. His father was a railway clerk in Montgomery, Alabama. Percy Julian left the family to enter DePauw University in Indiana. When he graduated as valedictorian of his class, his family was delighted. They were determined to give the same opportunity to the other children in the family. So Mrs. Julian moved to Greencastle, Indiana, with her three daughters and two sons. Mr. Julian remained in Montgomery and sent the necessary money so that the young people could have a college education. Their hopes and ambitions were realized. Both of Percy Julian's brothers became doctors, and each of his three sisters earned a Master's degree.

After his graduation from DePauw, Percy Julian received a scholarship to study at Harvard University, where he earned the degree of Master of Science. He then attended the University of Vienna in Austria, where he earned a Ph.D. After teaching a number of years at DePauw, he entered the field of chemical research. He became the director of research for a large firm in Chicago. In 1953, he formed his own company, the Julian Laboratories. This company produced hormones, products from soy beans, and various drugs. After the first year of operation, the Julian Laboratories showed a profit of exactly $71.70. After the second year, however, the profit was an impressive $97,000, and these earnings have continued to increase. Percy Julian's contribution to American science has been great. His name has been listed for many years in *Who's Who in America*.

Law

Modern Negro lawyers have been active in protecting Negro rights. Nationally known lawyers have worked with such organizations as the NAACP in advancing the Negro's cause. Thurgood Marshall's work in overcoming segregation in public schools was described earlier in this chapter. He went on to become a federal judge in the United States Court of Appeals for the Second Circuit. In 1965, he became the Solicitor General for the United States, the first Negro to serve in this capacity. As he took the oath of office in the White House, President Lyndon Johnson had high praise for him: "Mr. Marshall symbolizes what is best in our society: the belief that human rights must be satisfied through the orderly processes of law." In June, 1967, President Johnson bestowed an even higher honor on Thurgood Marshall by appointing him to the United States Supreme Court, thus making him the first Negro Justice of the highest court in the land.

William Hastie's talent and training prepared him for a career of service as judge and government official. After taking his legal training at the Harvard University Law School, Mr. Hastie received his first federal appointment from President Franklin Roosevelt. He served as Assistant Solicitor in the Department of Interior. In 1937, he was appointed as a United States District Judge for the Virgin Islands. Resigning from this position in 1939, he became Dean of the Law School at Howard University in Washington, D.C.

William Hastie's career was developing during the crisis years of World War II. In 1940, he was once more appointed to serve in a federal position. He became a civilian aide to the Secretary of War. While he held this position, he worked unceasingly for integration in the armed forces. In 1944, William Hastie was appointed Governor of the Virgin Islands. The high point in his distinguished career came in 1949 when he became Judge of the United States Circuit Court of Appeals, Third Circuit. This was the highest judicial office that had been held by a Negro, up to this time.

Religion

The church has always been an important force in the Negro community. It has often done more than provide religious and moral leadership. Negro churches, particularly in large cities, have given practical help in their community. Some churches organized summer camps, playgrounds, family counseling services, or evening industrial schools. Others became centers for political action. The church also provided many opportunities for developing Negro leaders. Some ministers are well known for their leadership outside the church.

The man who founded the largest Negro church in the United States was Adam Clayton Powell, Sr. He retired from the ministry of his Abyssinian Baptist Church in New York in 1937, when the church had a membership of 15,000 persons. During his twenty-nine years as pastor, Mr. Powell had made the Abyssinian Church an active influence in Harlem life. In the depression years, the church helped thousands of jobless and hungry people. It gave coal, clothing, and medicines to the needy. A food kitchen was opened in the gymnasium of the church's community house, and approximately two thousand people were fed there every day.

Politics

Adam Clayton Powell, Jr., took over the leadership of his father's Abyssinian Baptist Church in 1937. In 1944 he was elected to Congress as the first Negro Representative from the East. Still representing New York at Washington in 1961, Powell became Chairman of the Education and Labor Committee of the House of Representatives. In 1966, Powell was charged with contempt of court for failure to pay the assessment in a libel case which he had lost earlier. He came under further criticism for his use of public funds. Early in 1967 he lost his committee chairmanship and in March of the same year the House voted to exclude him from his seat in Congress. At a special election in April, he was voted back into Congress by his constituency.

Carl Rowan was named Deputy Assistant Secretary of State for Public Affairs in 1961. In 1963 he was appointed ambassador to Finland and, in 1964, Director of the United States Information Agency. In 1965 he joined the Marshall Field chain of newspapers as a syndicated columnist.

The elections of 1966 produced two more firsts for Negroes in politics. Lucius Amerson of Macon County, Alabama, became the first Negro sheriff in the South since Reconstruction days. Edward W. Brooke won the first U.S. Senate seat to be held by a Negro since Reconstruction Days. Brooke, who grew up in a middle-class home in Washington where his father was a Veteran's Administration lawyer, was formerly State Attorney General in Massachusetts and represents that state in Washington.

Foreign Service

Ambassadors to foreign countries serve as representatives of our government wherever they are stationed. Appointed to their position by the President of the United States, they have a respon-

Edward W. Brooke

sible role in government service. To date, not many Negroes have represented the United States as ambassadors to foreign nations. In recent years, Edward Dudley served as Minister to Liberia from 1949 to 1953. In 1953 Jesse Locker replaced him as Ambassador to Liberia.

In 1965 President Johnson selected a Negro lawyer, Mrs. Patricia Roberts Harris, as Ambassador to Luxembourg. Other Negro ambassadors serving in 1965 included Mercer Cook, Senegal; Clinton Knox, Dahomey; Hugh Smythe, Syria; Franklin Williams, Ghana; Elliott P. Skinner, Upper Volta; and James Nabrit, Jr., United States Mission to the United Nations. Mr. Nabrit resigned from his diplomatic post in 1967 to return to the presidency of Howard University.

Business

America's wealth is tied to the development of industry and business. Since World War II, many different jobs have been opened to Negroes for the first time. Qualified men and women have become stewardesses and pilots. They have worked in television studios as actors, stage managers, and cameramen. They have been employed as chemists and engineers in large industrial companies. Some have started and operated thriving businesses of their own.

In North Carolina, Charles Clinton Spaulding started to work in a small life insurance company. His untiring efforts caused the firm to grow into the huge North Carolina Mutual Life Insurance Company. Spaulding himself served as president of the company from 1923 until his death in 1952.

In Birmingham, Alabama, Arthur Gaston rose from a three-dollar-a-day laborer to a millionaire owner of several successful businesses. His business enterprises have included an insurance company, a chain of funeral homes, a business college, a chain of motels, a housing development, a savings and loan association, a realty and investment corporation, and a cemetery.

One of the most successful business ventures of recent years has been the development of Negro magazines. The *Negro Digest, Jet,* and *Ebony* all owe their existence to the efforts of John Johnson. Born in 1919, John Johnson spent his early life under conditions of great poverty. His family moved to Chicago when the boy was of high school age. He worked hard at school, determined to take advantage of every opportunity. He was editor of the school newspaper, president of the student council, and manager of the yearbook. He was also a tireless reader, studying particularly the lives of Negro leaders.

After high school, John Johnson worked for a while in an insurance company in Chicago. In 1942, with borrowed money, he started his career in the publishing business. He printed the *Negro Digest,* a small magazine about Negro affairs. The new magazine was an immediate success and by 1943, over fifty thousand copies were sold every month.

In 1945, *Ebony* made its appearance. This magazine contained stories emphasizing the achievement and success of Negroes. Articles about Negro history have pointed out their continuing contributions to American life. This magazine has a circulation which reaches into the hundreds of thousands every month. After the success of *Ebony,* the Johnson Publishing Company started printing three more magazines: *Jet, Hue,* and *Tan.*

John Johnson's remarkable career as a self-made man has left him with an appreciation of the United States as a land of opportunity. In one interview he expressed his feeling that the United States is the world's best home for Negroes.

A wounded medic aids a fellow soldier in Viet Nam.

Conclusion

The Negro's record in American life has been long and exciting. The history of the race is rich in achievement and constant efforts to overcome barriers of prejudice. It has been a story of both abrupt and gradual changes. Racial discrimination is gone from many areas of American life, but not from all. Today's newspapers describe the challenges being made against existing barriers. What occurs now will become tomorrow's history, for history is a living thing, an account of the events that affect our present and future lives.

The history of the Negro American is an important part of the history of our entire nation. The development of the United States has been profoundly influenced by the Negro and his position in America. Negro slavery provided the manpower for the plantation system of agriculture in the South. The lives of whites, as well as Negroes, became tightly bound to this rural way of life. Later, westward expansion into new territories raised the question whether or not the new states were to permit slavery. The Civil War, which started as an effort to keep the country united, brought about the end of slavery. Historic documents, like the Emancipation Proclamation and the Thirteenth, Fourteenth, and Fifteenth Amendments to the Constitution, defined Negro citizenship and became a part of the American heritage. Court decisions and laws dealt with Negro rights and brought changes to traditional patterns of living. In recent years, thousands of people have organized to end racial discrimination and the prejudice from which it stems.

The history of any nation pays tribute to its leaders and heroes. The United States has been enriched by a variety of contributions from prominent Negro citizens. Throughout the years, individuals with talent and determination have reached new goals of excellence in many areas of American culture: education, religion, literature, art, music, sports, entertainment, politics, government, business, science, and law. In many cases, these persons were the Negro pioneers in their chosen work, the first of their race to earn recognition for outstanding achievement. In overcoming handicaps of prejudice, the talented leaders succeeded in opening unseen doors of opportunity. By their courage and efforts, they made it easier for others to follow in their footsteps. Through their talents and skills, they built greater understanding and respect among all American citizens.

Some Important Events in Negro History

1492 • Alonzo Pietro, captain of the *Niña,* sailed with Columbus' expedition to America. Pietro is identified as a Negro by some historians.

1513 • Thirty Negroes were a part of Balboa's expedition, which crossed Panama and discovered the Pacific Ocean.

1519 • The army of Hernando Cortez conquered the Aztec Indians in Mexico. Negroes were a part of this expedition.

1539 • Estevan, or Stephen (also called Estevanico, or Little Steven), explored the western regions of North America through what is now Arizona and New Mexico.

1619 • Twenty Africans arrived at Jamestown, Virginia, and became indentured servants.

1624 • William Tucker was born. He was the first Negro child to be born in the land that was later to become the United States.

1663 • First serious slave conspiracy of Negro slaves and white indentured servants in Gloucester County, Virginia. The plot was betrayed by a house servant.

1731 • Benjamin Banneker, mathematician, astronomer, and one of the planners of Washington, D.C., was born in Maryland.

1760 • Richard Allen, a founder of the African Methodist Episcopal Church, was born a slave in Philadelphia.

1762 • James Derham, first American Negro doctor, was born in Philadelphia.

1770 • March 5. The Boston Massacre occurred. Crispus Attucks and four other colonists were killed by British soldiers.

1773 • Phillis Wheatley's book, *Poems on Various Subjects, Religious and Moral,* was published.

1775 · Negro soldiers fought in the Battles of Lexington and Concord. Later they took part in the Battle of Bunker Hill.

1777 · Vermont abolished slavery within its borders. It was the first state to do so.

1787 · The Free African Society was organized in Philadelphia by Richard Allen and Absolem Jones.
      · The Northwest Ordinance prohibited slavery within the Northwest Territory.

1793 · The Fugitive Slave Law was passed by Congress, making it unlawful to harbor a runaway slave.

1794 · Richard Allen and others organized the Bethel African Methodist Episcopal Church.

1797 · Sojourner Truth, leading Negro abolitionist, was born a slave in Hurley, New York.

1800 · Gabriel Prosser planned his unsuccessful slave revolt.
      · Nat Turner, a later leader of a slave revolt, was born in Virginia.

1814 · Negro troops, as well as white, fought in the Battle of New Orleans under the command of General Andrew Jackson.

1817 · Frederick Douglass, abolitionist, lecturer, and author, was born a slave in Maryland.

1822 · Denmark Vesey organized a slave rebellion in Charleston, South Carolina. The plans were revealed to authorities, and the revolt did not take place.

1826 · John Russwurm, first Negro college graduate in the United States, received his degree from Bowdoin College.

1827 · *Freedom's Journal,* first Negro newspaper, was published in New York. John Russwurm and Samuel Cornish were the editors.

1831 · William Lloyd Garrison's newspaper, the *Liberator,* first appeared.
      · Nat Turner's rebellion took place. Fifty-seven persons were killed before Turner was captured and put to death.

1839 · Robert Smalls, hero of the Civil War and Reconstruction Congressman, was born a slave in South Carolina.

1841 · Blanche Kelso Bruce, future United States Senator and first Negro to serve a full term, was born a slave in Virginia.

1847 · First copy of the *North Star,* Frederick Douglass' newspaper, appeared.

1849 · Harriet Tubman escaped from slavery in Maryland. She later led over 300 slaves to freedom on the Underground Railroad.

1852 · March 20. Harriet Beecher Stowe's novel, *Uncle Tom's Cabin,* was published.

1856 · Booker T. Washington, famous educator and Negro leader, was born a slave in Virginia.
· Wilberforce University was founded in Ohio.

1857 · The Dred Scott decision was given by the Supreme Court. This decision ruled that Negroes were not citizens.

1859 · John Brown led the raid against Harpers Ferry in Virginia.

1862 · Robert Smalls, slave sailor of South Carolina, delivered the Confederate warship *Planter* into the hands of the Union Navy.

1863 · January 1. President Lincoln issued the Emancipation Proclamation.

1865 · The Freedmen's Bureau was established to help refugees and freed slaves.
· December 18. The Thirteenth Amendment to the Constitution, which abolished slavery in the United States, was adopted.

1866 · Fisk University was opened in Nashville, Tennessee.

1867 · Howard University was opened in Washington, D.C.
· Morehouse College was founded in Atlanta.
· The Ku Klux Klan held its first national meeting at Nashville, Tennessee.

1868 · William Edward Burghardt Du Bois, scholar and Negro leader, was born in Great Barrington, Massachusetts.
· Hampton Institute was opened in Virginia.
· July 28. The Fourteenth Amendment to the Constitution, which legally granted citizenship to Negroes, was adopted.

1870 · Hiram Revels became the first Negro member of the United States Senate. He succeeded Jefferson Davis as the Congressman from Mississippi.
· March 30. The Fifteenth Amendment to the Constitution, which granted the right to vote to Negroes, was adopted.

1871 · The Jubilee Singers of Fisk University started on their first concert tour.

1872 · Paul Laurence Dunbar, poet, was born in Dayton, Ohio.

1875 · Mary McLeod Bethune, educator, was born in South Carolina.

1877 · Frederick Douglass was appointed Marshal of the District of Columbia.
· Henry O. Flipper became the first Negro to be graduated from West Point.

1881 · Booker T. Washington started Tuskegee Institute.
· The Jim Crow railroad car law of Tennessee began the segregation movement.

1891 · The first training school for Negro nurses was established at Provident Hospital in Chicago.

1893 · Dr. Daniel Hale Williams performed the first successful heart operation in Chicago.

1896 · The Supreme Court ruled on the *Plessy vs. Ferguson* case. Its decision upheld the separate-but-equal theory in regard to railroad transportation.

1904 · Ralph Bunche, educator and diplomat, was born in Detroit, Michigan.

1905 · The Niagara Movement was started by a group of Negro intellectuals. W. E. B. Du Bois was one of the leaders.

1909 · The NAACP was organized in New York City.
· The North Pole was reached by Robert E. Peary and his Negro assistant Matthew Henson.

1910 · The National Urban League was organized in New York City.

1915 · The "grandfather clause" was ruled unconstitutional by the Supreme Court.
· Carter Woodson founded the Association for the Study of Negro Life and History.

1920 · Marcus Garvey's Black Nationalist movement, the Universal Improvement Association, held a national convention in New York. The meeting attracted some 25,000 Negroes.

1922 · *Harlem Shadows,* a volume of poetry by Claude McKay, was published.

1925 · Countee Cullen's *Color* and Alain Locke's *The New Negro* were published.

1929 · Martin Luther King, Jr., civil rights leader, was born in Atlanta, Georgia.

1936 · Jesse Owens set three track records and captured four gold medals at the Olympic Games held in Berlin, Germany.
· Mary McLeod Bethune was appointed director of Negro affairs for the National Youth Administration.

1937 · William Hastie was appointed judge of the Federal District Court in the Virgin Islands. He was the first Negro to serve as a federal judge.
· Joe Louis became the heavyweight boxing champion of the world.

1940 · James Bland's song, *Carry Me Back to Ole Virginny,* was named the official song of Virginia by action of the state legislature.
· Benjamin O. Davis, Sr., became the first Negro general in the United States Army.
· Dr. Charles Drew became medical director of the British blood plasma program.

1941 · President Franklin Roosevelt issued Executive Order 8802, which banned racial discrimination in defense industries.
· Dorie Miller, Navy messman, manned a machine gun for the first time in his life to defend the battleship *Arizona* at Pearl Harbor.

1942 · The Congress of Racial Equality (CORE) was organized in New York.

1943 · A series of serious race riots took place in Los Angeles, Detroit, Harlem, and Beaumont, Texas.

1947 · Jackie Robinson, first Negro in major league baseball, played with the Brooklyn Dodgers.

1948 · President Harry Truman issued Executive Order 9981, which banned racial discrimination in the armed forces.
· Ralph Bunche became Acting Mediator for the United Nations in Palestine.

1949 · Wesley A. Brown became the first Negro graduate of Annapolis Naval Academy.
· William Hastie was appointed judge of the United States Circuit Court of Appeals.

1950 · Gwendolyn Brooks was awarded the Pulitzer Prize for Poetry.
· Ralph Bunche was awarded the Nobel Peace Prize.

1952 · Tuskegee Institute reported that for the first time in seventy-one years there were no lynchings.

1954 • The Supreme Court ruled on the *Brown vs. the Board of Education of Topeka, Kansas* case. This decision banned racial discrimination in public education.
  • Benjamin O. Davis, Jr., became the first Negro general in the United States Air Force.

1955 • Marian Anderson made her Metropolitan Opera debut in Verdi's *Masked Ball.* She was the first Negro to sing with the company.
  • December 5. The bus boycott in Montgomery, Alabama, began.

1957 • The Southern Christian Leadership Conference (SCLC) was organized under the leadership of Dr. Martin Luther King, Jr.
  • Althea Gibson became the women's tennis champion.

1960 • Sit-ins were started in Greensboro, North Carolina, by four college students.
  • The Student Non-Violent Coordinating Committee (SNCC) was organized.
  • Elijah Muhammad, Black Nationalist leader, called for the creation of a Negro state.

1961 • Robert Weaver was appointed Administrator of the Housing and Home Finance Agency.
  • "Freedom Riders" organized bus rides through the South.
  • Thurgood Marshall became judge of the United States Court of Appeals.

1962 • James Meredith became the first Negro to attend classes at the University of Mississippi.

1963 • August 28. The March on Washington was attended by two hundred thousand people who wanted to dramatize their wish for equal rights for all citizens.

1964 • The Civil Rights Act was passed by the Congress of the United States.
  • Serious race riots broke out in Harlem, Chicago, Philadelphia, and other northern cities.
  • Dr. Martin Luther King, Jr., was awarded the Nobel Peace Prize.

1965 • Dr. Martin Luther King, Jr., led a march from Selma to Montgomery, Alabama, to urge Negro voter registration in the South.

- Mrs. Patricia Harris was appointed United States Ambassador to Luxembourg by President Johnson.
- The Voting Rights Act was passed by Congress, granting equal voting opportunities to all citizens.

1966 • Robert Weaver was appointed Secretary of Housing and Urban Development. He is the first Negro to serve in the President's cabinet.
- James Meredith, shot while walking from Memphis, Tennessee, to Jackson, Mississippi, in a personal effort to urge Negro voter registration in the South, temporarily gave up his walk. Other Civil Rights leaders and workers took over for him.

1967 • Thurgood Marshall was appointed to the United States Supreme Court. He is the first Negro to serve as a Justice of the highest court in the country.

Some Important Statistics in Negro History

TABLE A

Percentage of Negroes in the Total Population of the United States, 1790–1960

Year	Total Population	Whites	Negroes	Negro Percentage in Total Population
1790	3,929,000	3,172,000	757,000	19.3
1800	5,297,000	4,306,000	1,002,000	18.9
1820	9,638,000	7,867,000	1,772,000	18.4
1840	17,120,000	14,196,000	2,874,000	16.8
1860	31,513,000	26,923,000	4,442,000	14.1
1880	50,262,000	43,403,000	6,581,000	13.1
1900	76,094,000	66,809,000	8,834,000	11.6
1920	106,466,000	94,821,000	10,463,000	9.8
1940	132,122,000	118,215,000	12,866,000	9.7
1960	180,684,000	158,832,000	18,872,000	10.5

Adapted from Lerone Bennett, *Before the Mayflower: A History of the Negro in America 1619–1962* (Chicago: Johnson Publishing Co., 1962), pp. 335 ff.; and Bureau of the Census, *Historical Statistics of the United States, Colonial Times to 1957*, Series A. 1–3 (Washington, D.C.: Government Printing Office, 1960), p. 7.

T A B L E   B

Distribution of Negroes in the United States

At every census from 1790–1900, at least 90 percent of the Negro population of the United States lived in the South. After 1910, Negroes began to move from the South to the North and West.

Year	Percentage of Negroes in the South	Percentage of Negroes in the North and West
1910	89%	11%
1920	85%	15%
1940	77%	23%
1960	60%	40%

Adapted from John P. Davis, ed., *The American Negro Reference Book* (Englewood Cliffs, N.J.: Prentice-Hall, 1966), p. 102–104.

After 1910, Negroes began to move from rural to urban areas.

Year	Percentage of Negroes in Rural Areas	Percentage of Negroes in Urban Areas
1910	73%	27%
1960	27%	73%

This move from rural to urban areas was more pronounced among Negroes than among whites, who also moved from rural to urban areas.

Year	Percentage of Whites in Rural Areas	Percentage of Whites in Urban Areas
1910	52%	48%
1960	30%	70%

Adapted from Philip M. Hauser, "Demographic Factors in the Integration of the Negro," in Talcott Parsons, and Kenneth B. Clark, eds., *The Negro American* (Boston: Houghton Mifflin, 1966), p. 75.

Bibliography

Introduction

Handlin, Oscar. *The Uprooted*. Boston: Little, Brown and Company, 1952.

Kennedy, John F. *A Nation of Immigrants*. New York: Harper and Row, Publishers, 1964.

Lerner, Max. *America as a Civilization*. New York: Simon and Schuster, 1957.

Yinger, J. Milton. *A Minority Group in American Society*. New York: McGraw-Hill, Inc., 1965.

The African Background

Bennett, Lerone. *Before the Mayflower: A History of the Negro in America*. Chicago: The Johnson Publishing Company, Inc., 1962.

Franklin, John Hope. *From Slavery to Freedom*. New York: Alfred A. Knopf, Inc., 1961.

Rotberg, Robert. *A Political History of Tropical Africa*. New York: Harcourt, Brace & World, Inc., 1965.

Woodson, Carter Godwin. *The Negro in Our History*. Washington, D.C.: The Associated Publishers, Inc., 1938.

Woodson, Carter, and Wesley, Charles. *The Story of the Negro Retold*. Washington, D.C.: The Associated Publishers, Inc., 1959.

Exploration and Colonization

Bennett, Lerone. *Before the Mayflower: A History of the Negro in America*. Chicago: The Johnson Publishing Company, Inc., 1962.

Eppse, Merl R. *The Negro Too in American History*. Nashville: The National Publishing Company, 1943.

Franklin, John Hope. *From Slavery to Freedom*. New York: Alfred A. Knopf, Inc., 1961.

Woodson, Carter Godwin. *Negro Makers of History*. Washington, D.C.: The Associated Publishers, Inc., 1938.

The Revolutionary War Era

Adams, Russell L. *Great Negroes Past and Present.* Chicago: Afro-Am Publishing Company, Inc., 1964.

Bardolph, Richard. *The Negro Vanguard.* New York: Rinehart and Company, Inc., 1959.

Bennett, Lerone. *Before the Mayflower: A History of the Negro in America.* Chicago: The Johnson Publishing Company, Inc., 1962.

Franklin, John Hope. *From Slavery to Freedom.* New York: Alfred A. Knopf, Inc., 1961.

Matthews, Marcia, *Richard Allen.* Baltimore: Helicon Press, Inc., 1963.

Quarles, Benjamin. *The Negro in the American Revolution.* Chapel Hill, North Carolina: The University of North Carolina Press, 1961.

Woodson, Carter Godwin. *Negro Makers of History.* Washington, D.C.: The Associated Publishers, Inc., 1938.

From Revolutionary War to Civil War

Adams, Russell L. *Great Negroes Past and Present.* Chicago: Afro-Am Publishing Company, Inc., 1964.

American Oil Company. *American Travelers Guide to Negro History.* Chicago: American Oil Company, 1963.

Bardolph, Richard. *The Negro Vanguard.* New York: Rinehart and Company, Inc., 1959.

Beckwourth, James P. *The Life and Adventures of James P. Beckwourth.* New York: Alfred A. Knopf, Inc., 1931.

Burns, W. Haywood. *Voices of Negro Protest in America.* New York: The Oxford University Press, 1963.

Douglass, Frederick. *The Life and Times of Frederick Douglass.* New York: Collier Books, Revised, 1962.

Embree, Edwin R. *Brown Americans.* New York: Viking Press, 1943.

Eppse, Merl R. *The Negro Too in American History.* Nashville: The National Publishing Company, 1943.

Franklin, John Hope. *From Slavery to Freedom.* New York: Alfred A. Knopf, Inc., 1961.

Redding, Saunders. *The Lonesome Road.* Garden City, New York: Doubleday and Company, Inc., 1958.

Stampp, Kenneth Milton. *The Peculiar Institution: Slavery in the Ante-bellum South.* New York: Alfred A. Knopf, Inc., 1956.

Sterling, Dorothy. *Freedom Train: The Story of Harriet Tubman.* Garden City, New York: Doubleday and Company, Inc, 1954.

Woodson, Carter Godwin. *Negro Makers of History.* Washington, D.C.: The Associated Publishers, Inc., 1938.

The Civil War

Adams, Russell L. *Great Negroes Past and Present.* Chicago: Afro-Am Publishing Company, Inc., 1964.

Bardolph, Richard. *The Negro Vanguard.* New York: Rinehart and Company, Inc., 1959.

Douglass, Frederick. *The Life and Times of Frederick Douglass.* New York: Collier Books, Revised, 1962.

Embree, Edwin R. *Brown Americans.* New York: Viking Press, 1943.

Eppse, Merl R. *The Negro Too in American History.* Nashville: The National Publishing Company, 1943.

Franklin, John Hope. *From Slavery to Freedom.* New York: Alfred A. Knopf, Inc., 1961.

Quarles, Benjamin. *The Negro in the Civil War.* Boston: Little, Brown and Company, 1953.

Reconstruction Days

Douglass, Frederick. *The Life and Times of Frederick Douglass.* New York: Collier Books, Revised, 1962.

Franklin, John Hope. *From Slavery to Freedom.* New York: Alfred A. Knopf, Inc., 1961.

Frazier, Edward Franklin. *The Negro in the United States.* New York: The Macmillan Company, 1957.

Tussman, Joseph (ed.). *The Supreme Court on Racial Discrimination.* New York: Oxford University Press, 1963.

Woodson, Carter Godwin. *Negro Makers of History.* Washington, D.C.: The Associated Publishers, Inc., 1938.

Woodson, Carter, and Wesley, Charles. *The Story of the Negro Retold.* Washington, D.C.: The Associated Publishers, Inc., 1959.

Woodward, C. Vann. *The Strange Career of Jim Crow.* New York: The Oxford Press, 1955.

After Reconstruction: 1875–1900

Adams, Russell L. *Great Negroes Past and Present*. Chicago: Afro-Am Publishing Company, Inc., 1964.

Bardolph, Richard. *The Negro Vanguard*. New York: Rinehart and Company, Inc., 1959.

Bennett, Lerone. *Before the Mayflower: A History of the Negro in America*. Chicago: The Johnson Publishing Company, Inc., 1962.

Bontemps, Arna. *100 Years of Negro Freedom*. New York: Dodd, Mead and Company, 1962.

Buckler, Helen. *Dr. Dan, Pioneer American Surgeon*. Boston: Little, Brown and Company, 1954.

Butcher, Margaret Just. *The Negro in American Culture*. New York: Alfred A. Knopf, Inc., 1956.

Porter, James A. *Modern Negro Art*. New York: Dryden Press, 1943.

Redding, Saunders. *The Lonesome Road*. Garden City, New York: Doubleday and Company, Inc., 1958.

Washington, Booker T. *Up from Slavery*. Garden City, New York: Doubleday and Company, Inc., 1901.

Early Twentieth Century: 1900–1929

Adams, Russell. *Great Negroes Past and Present*. Chicago: Afro-Am Publishing Company, Inc., 1964.

Anderson, Marian. *My Lord, What a Morning*. New York: Viking Press, 1963.

Bailey, Helen Miller. *Forty American Biographies*. New York: Harcourt, Brace and World, Inc., 1964.

Bardolph, Richard. *The Negro Vanguard*. New York: Rinehart and Company, Inc., 1959.

Bennett, Lerone. *Before the Mayflower: A History of the Negro in America*. Chicago: The Johnson Publishing Company, Inc., 1962.

Bontemps, Arna. *100 Years of Negro Freedom*. New York: Dodd, Mead and Company, 1962.

Butcher, Margaret Just. *The Negro in American Culture*. New York: Alfred A. Knopf, Inc., 1956.

Du Bois, W. E. B. *The Souls of Black Folk*. Greenwich, Connecticut: Fawcett Publications, Inc., 1961.

Embree, Edwin R. *Brown Americans.* New York: Viking Press, 1943.

Holt, Rackham. *Mary McLeod Bethune.* Garden City, New York: Doubleday and Company, Inc., 1964.

Johnson, James Weldon. *Along This Way.* New York: Viking Press, 1933.

Locke, Alain. *The New Negro: An Interpretation.* New York: Albert and Charles Boni Publishers, 1925.

Richardson, Ben Albert. *Great American Negroes.* New York: Crowell Publishers, 1945.

The Depression and World War II: 1929–1945

Bardolph, Richard. *The Negro Vanguard.* New York: Rinehart and Company, Inc., 1959.

Franklin, John Hope. *From Slavery to Freedom.* New York: Alfred A. Knopf, Inc., 1961.

Ottley, Roi. *New World A-Coming.* Boston: Houghton Mifflin Company, 1943.

Richardson, Ben Albert. *Great American Negroes.* New York: Crowell Publishers, 1945.

The Search for Equality: 1945–1966

Adams, Russell L. *Great Negroes Past and Present.* Chicago: Afro-Am Publishing Company, Inc., 1964.

Bardolph, Richard. *The Negro Vanguard.* New York: Rinehart and Company, Inc., 1959.

Burns, W. Haywood. *Voices of Negro Protest in America.* New York: Oxford University Press, 1963.

Butcher, Margaret Just. *The Negro in American Culture.* New York: Alfred A. Knopf, Inc., 1956.

Clark, Kenneth B. *The Negro Protest.* Boston: The Beacon Press, 1963.

Davis, John P. (ed.). *The American Negro Reference Book.* Englewood Cliffs, New Jersey: Prentice-Hall, Inc., 1966.

King, Martin Luther, Jr. *Why We Can't Wait.* New York: Harper and Row, Publishers, 1964.

Ottley, Roi. *New World A-Coming.* Boston: Houghton Mifflin Company, 1943.

Parsons, Talcott, and Kenneth B. Clark (eds.). *The Negro American.* Boston: Houghton Mifflin Company, 1966.

Salk, Erwin A. (ed.). *The Layman's Guide to Negro History.* Chicago: Quadrangle Paperback, 1966.

Tussman, Joseph (ed.). *The Supreme Court on Racial Discrimination.* New York: Oxford University Press, 1963.

White, Walter. *A Man Called White.* New York: Viking Press, 1948.

Young, Whitney M. *To Be Free.* New York: McGraw-Hill, Inc., 1964.

Index